PRAISE FOR *CREATED TO HEAR GOD*

"Havilah is the little sister I never had. She's fierce and kind, and she has a gift for demystifying spiritual topics with her 'let's get real' approach. If you're out there wondering if God still speaks and if He wants to speak to you, this is your book. Havilah unpacks the truth that God is always speaking and equips you with practical tools so you can recognize His voice like you would recognize the voice of a friend. I'm a firm believer that God wants to talk to you more than you want to hear from Him. Grab this book, a pen, and a journal, and get ready to hear from Him."

—LISA BEVERE, *NEW YORK TIMES* BESTSELLING AUTHOR OF
GODMOTHERS, WITHOUT RIVAL, AND *LIONESS ARISING*

"There are certain subjects in the church that feel like they've been elevated so high, they've become unreachable. Being led by the spirit is one of those, even though it's meant to be a normal part of life for every believer. That's why I'm thrilled Havilah has brought us this book, *Created to Hear God*, to teach us how to discern the voice of God and be led by the spirit. Havilah is one of the most gifted communicators I know. Her stories and insights, laced with fabulous humor, are just as impactful as they are practical. I believe this book will be a source of inspiration and encouragement for everyone who reads it."

—BILL JOHNSON, SENIOR PASTOR OF BETHEL CHURCH AND AUTHOR OF
WHEN HEAVEN INVADES EARTH, GOD IS GOOD, AND *THE RESTING PLACE*

"I am so grateful for Havilah's trusted and prophetic voice. She is not only committed to helping us understand this vital spiritual gift, but teaches us how to exercise it with compassion, integrity, and wisdom."

—CHRISTINE CAINE, BESTSELLING AUTHOR AND
FOUNDER OF A21 AND PROPEL WOMEN

"God wants to speak to you! You don't have to be a seminary student to hear His voice. You don't have to be a worship leader, teacher, preacher, or evangelist either. I love how Havilah has taken something that feels like it's reserved for only the most spiritual and made it accessible to anyone who wants it."

—BIANCA JUAREZ OLTHOFF, PASTOR, PODCASTER, AND
BESTSELLING AUTHOR OF *GRIT DON'T QUIT*

"Sitting down with Havilah is like being treated by a spiritual audiologist. Every time I'm with her, I walk away hearing God's voice more clearly! I can pretty much guarantee you'll feel the same way after making your way through the pages of this book. *Created to Hear God* cuts through the lofty language Christians often use and breaks things down in a way that feels accessible. This book is an invitation to step away from the static of our all-too-busy lives and focus on the Lover of our soul so we can experience the miracle of communing with Him."

–LISA HARPER, AUTHOR OF *A PERFECT MESS* AND *BELIEVING JESUS*

"Havilah's new book, *Created to Hear God*, uncomplicates the spiritual principle of our divine design and innate nature to hear the voice of God and gives practical insight for understanding how you were uniquely created to hear the voice of God. Havilah has been a daughter to me for several decades. I count it an honor to watch the Lord fan the flame within her to teach and equip a generation to step into the fullness of who they were created to be. This book is a representation of the revelatory and applicable message she carries for every believer that will be a catalyst to partnering with the voice of God in your life."

–KRIS VALLOTTON, SENIOR ASSOCIATE LEADER OF BETHEL CHURCH AND AUTHOR OF *THE SUPERNATURAL WAYS OF ROYALTY, SPIRITUAL INTELLIGENCE,* AND *UPRISING*

"Havilah is the real deal. I've known her for twenty-five years, and she is an authentic and powerful communicator who loves the word of God. My prayer for you as you read this book is that you'd hear God's voice more clearly and come to know Him more deeply. May her words inspire you to seek His voice and run after Him with all you have."

–JENN JOHNSON, WORSHIP LEADER, SONGWRITER, AND PRESIDENT OF BETHEL MUSIC

"I am so happy Havilah wrote this book. Too often we overcomplicate things like hearing God's voice and being led by Him, leaving us confused and doubting, instead of moving forward into all that He has for us. In this practical guidebook, Havilah gives us the tools we need to discern the voice of God so we can walk in even deeper relationship with Him."

–REAL TALK KIM, SENIOR PASTOR AT LIMITLESS CHURCH AND AUTHOR OF *YOU GOTTA GET UP!*

"People are hungry for really knowing God and hearing His voice. We are hearing people from all walks of life share their encounters with God and hearing His voice, everywhere from music legend Dolly Parton to former vice president Mike Pence to celebrities like Denzel Washington. This is one of the pressing themes in culture right now, but there is a gap between sound biblical teaching that can activate this more in your life, and just having belief that it 'could' happen. That is where Havilah's expertise comes in. In *Created to Hear God* she expertly and theologically examines the prophetic personality types in the Bible. You will find yourself in these pages. Even better, this will be a new tool that is exactly on time for your own journey in hearing God and understanding his process in your life and for those around you."

**—SHAWN BOLZ, PRESIDENT OF BOLZ MINISTRIES
AND AUTHOR OF *TRANSLATING GOD***

"Havilah is one of my favorite storytellers. Her comedic timing is only matched by her ability to gently expose the human condition in all its grit and glory with a wink. She delivers truth in a way that makes you feel an immense sense of clarity, belonging, and camaraderie. If you've felt a longing in your heart to draw near to your Creator and hear His voice, this book is bound to give you the tools you've been looking for."

—AMANDA COOK, SINGER AND SONGWRITER

CREATED TO HEAR GOD

CREATED TO HEAR GOD

4 UNIQUE AND PROVEN WAYS TO CONFIDENTLY DISCERN HIS VOICE

HAVILAH CUNNINGTON

NELSON
BOOKS

An Imprint of Thomas Nelson

Created to Hear God

Copyright © 2023 by Havilah Cunnington

Published in Nashville, Tennessee, by Nelson Books, an imprint of Thomas Nelson. Nelson Books and Thomas Nelson are registered trademarks of HarperCollins Christian Publishing, Inc.

The author is represented by Alive Literary Agency, www.aliveliterary.com.

Thomas Nelson titles may be purchased in bulk for educational, business, fundraising, or sales promotional use. For information, please email SpecialMarkets@ThomasNelson.com.

Unless otherwise noted, Scripture quotations are taken from The Holy Bible, New International Version®, NIV®. Copyright © 1973, 1978, 1984, 2011 by Biblica, Inc.® Used by permission of Zondervan. All rights reserved worldwide. www.Zondervan.com. The "NIV" and "New International Version" are trademarks registered in the United States Patent and Trademark Office by Biblica, Inc.®

Scripture quotations marked AMP are taken from the Amplified® Bible (AMP). Copyright © 2015 by The Lockman Foundation. Used by permission. www.Lockman.org.

Scripture quotations marked AMPC are taken from the Amplified® Bible (AMPC). Copyright © 1954, 1958, 1962, 1964, 1965, 1987 by The Lockman Foundation. Used by permission. www.Lockman.org.

Scripture quotations marked ERV are taken from the HOLY BIBLE: EASY-TO-READ VERSION ©2014 by Bible League International. Used by permission.

Scripture quotations marked ESV are taken from the ESV® Bible (The Holy Bible, English Standard Version®). Copyright © 2001 by Crossway, a publishing ministry of Good News Publishers. Used by permission. All rights reserved.

Scripture quotations marked MSG are taken from THE MESSAGE. Copyright © 1993, 2002, 2018 by Eugene H. Peterson. Used by permission of NavPress. All rights reserved. Represented by Tyndale House Publishers, Inc.

Scripture quotations marked NKJV are taken from the New King James Version®. Copyright © 1982 by Thomas Nelson. Used by permission. All rights reserved.

Scripture quotations marked NLT are taken from the Holy Bible, New Living Translation. Copyright © 1996, 2004, 2015 by Tyndale House Foundation. Used by permission of Tyndale House Ministries, Carol Stream, Illinois 60188. All rights reserved.

Scripture quotations marked RSV are taken from the Revised Standard Version of the Bible. Copyright © 1946, 1952, and 1971 National Council of the Churches of Christ in the United States of America. Used by permission. All rights reserved worldwide.

Scripture quotations marked VOICE are taken from The Voice™. © 2012 by Ecclesia Bible Society. Used by permission. All rights reserved. Note: Italics in quotations from The Voice are used to "indicate words not directly tied to the dynamic translation of the original language" but that "bring out the nuance of the original, assist in completing ideas, and . . . provide readers with information that would have been obvious to the original audience" (The Voice, preface).

Names and identifying characteristics of some individuals have been changed to preserve their privacy.

ISBN 978-1-4002-3863-7 (ePub)
ISBN 978-1-4002-3862-0 (HC)

Library of Congress Cataloging-in-Publication Data

Library of Congress Control Number: 2023943224

Printed in the United States of America

23 24 25 26 27 LBC 5 4 3 2 1

To my husband, Ben.
My favorite Feeler.

CONTENTS

CONTENTS

LIFELONG LISTENING

"The man who guards the gate opens the gate for the shepherd. And the sheep listen to the voice of the shepherd. He calls his own sheep, using their names, and he leads them out. He brings all of his sheep out. Then he goes ahead of them and leads them. The sheep follow him, because they know his voice. But sheep will never follow someone they don't know. They will run away from him, because they don't know his voice."

—JOHN 10:3–5 ERV

INTRODUCTION

"GOD SPOKE TO ME."

What comes to your mind when you hear someone make that claim?

Maybe you feel skeptical: "Wait a minute, did the Almighty actually have a direct, audible conversation with this person? Is that even a thing these days?"

Maybe a twinge of worry makes you take a step back: "Oh no, I hope this person isn't going to go all preachy and fanatical on me. I'm all for being spiritual, but let's keep it real and grounded."

The claim might spark offense: "Seriously? Everything we need to hear from God is right there in the Bible. End of story. Asking for more than that is just asking for trouble."

You might feel angry enough to shut down the announcement before it starts: "Oh no you don't. I'm not about to let you run over me with your manipulative power scheme!"

Envy might rise to the surface. Someone around you may be claiming that God talks to them, and you begin to wonder, *Hold on a minute! Why does everyone else luck out in this department except for me? What's the deal?*

But let me tell you, there's another reaction worth exploring—a profound sense of awe. Just think about it: the reality that God takes the time to communicate with us humans is mind-blowing! It's absolutely incredible. So, naturally, you're eager to know what He said. You're hungry for those divine messages.

How you react when someone claims they've heard God's voice often depends on what you know (or don't know) about that person. If it's your best friend making the claim, you might give them more credit than a random stranger. But here's the deal, regardless of your thoughts on the matter: The fact that you're reading this book tells me something pretty important about you. It tells me that deep down you're curious to find out if you're one of those special people designed to hear from the Divine.

Guess what? You're not wrong. You absolutely are! And I have a wealth of wisdom to share about what it means:

- You are included.
- You were created by God for a beautiful connection with Him.
- You have the ability to recognize and know His voice.

The truth is, God communicates with us. He specifically created and designed us to hear Him. As Jesus said, He calls us—His own sheep—individually and by name, leading us along our unique paths.

Now, when I talk about hearing God, of course I'm referring

to the ways He speaks to us through His Word and the authorities He has placed in our lives. But it goes beyond that, my friend. You may have been taught that we Christians aren't meant to hear God's voice directly and should seek His guidance solely through the Bible. While God's Word is the ultimate authority and any message we receive from God must align with it, the truth is that He has personal, specific things to say to each and every one of us, in addition to what is written in the Bible.

Also, He communicates with us in diverse and incredible ways. Unveiling how you best hear God in these other ways is the heart of this book. I'm here to guide you on this extraordinary journey of discovering and embracing the myriad ways God speaks to you.

So, my friend, get ready for an incredible journey. We're going to explore, learn, and grow together as we uncover the rich tapestry of divine communication. Let's find out how you can open up and receive the messages the Divine has in store for you. It's time to embrace the adventure of hearing God's voice in a whole new way!

———

If you'd known me when I was first learning to hear God's voice, you would have known my main focus wasn't on changing the world. Nope, it was all about getting some inside scoop on my future hubby. I wanted to know his name, recognize him at first sight, and get a sneak peek at when we'd finally meet. Can you blame me? I was curious!

I was convinced that hearing the voice of God would be the ultimate game changer in my life. I mean, who wouldn't want that, right? I thought I'd become this discerning leader, effortlessly navigating the perfect and righteous path while unveiling my hidden superhero role in helping and serving others. It was like having a secret access code to success and recognition, as if God would personally hand me a gold plaque that read, "Congratulations on discovering your unique purpose!" Talk about depth and meaning!

But wait, there's more! Hearing God's voice would be my own personal shield of knowledge and understanding, protecting my boundaries like an impenetrable force field. It would give me crystal clear guidance and reassurance, making me the Jedi Master of life's uncertainties. And let's not forget that God's voice would lead me on exciting adventures and fulfill all my wildest dreams! Relationships? *No problem!* With God's divine insights, I'd achieve inner peace and become the ultimate conflict resolver. I mean, who needs therapy when you've got the heavenly hotline? Yeah, hearing God's voice would be a total game changer. You get the picture.

But I had no idea this journey would lead me to where I am now, reaching and helping so many people (all while happily married!). I also didn't know how critical and life-changing it would be to have a constant connection to the voice of God. There is nothing like knowing you never again have to face life on your own, unable to access God's wisdom for any circumstance you might face.

I've spent the last twenty-five years learning, practicing, and mastering the art of hearing God's voice for myself and others. As the women's pastor at Bethel Church and the cofounder with my husband of our nonprofit ministry, Truth to Table, I'm humbled to have guided thousands of people through my Prophetic Personalities course, which is designed to lead people into a deep understanding of this truth: God is not silent—you just haven't been taught how *you* are uniquely created to hear Him.

That truth is so important I'm going to say it again: God made you with the capacity to hear His voice. But maybe, just maybe, the *way* He made you to hear isn't what you expect.

From the moment I learned how to hear God, I began to grasp that He really is always speaking. I began to experience the truth that He is all-knowing, all-powerful, and always available. Now you have the same opportunity!

I know from experience that some of you are raring to go right now. Feel free to dive right into chapter 1. But a few of you might need to stand on the shore for a few more minutes. That's all right. Maybe you're unsure whether it's possible for a person to hear God speak. Maybe you feel as if you're the only person you know who doesn't hear God's voice, while everyone around you has a direct line. Fear asks, *What if I still can't even after reading this book?*

Maybe you're a new Christian, still trying to understand how it all works, or perhaps you've been following Jesus for years but have never grasped what it means to hear Him speak to you and speak over your life. Maybe you worry God doesn't care about your needs or that He's too preoccupied to listen to what you have to say. Maybe you've always heard God's voice, but the people in your life who also love God *aren't* hearing Him, or don't hear Him the way you do, and you wonder why. Maybe you just can't shake the feeling that there's something more to your relationship with God, and it keeps you up at night.

When it comes to the voice of God, whatever you feel, think, wonder, or worry about, I assure you that you're not alone. If you've experienced any of the above, come with me into the following pages. We'll talk about all of it.

I'm going to teach you about the different ways in which God speaks to us based on our uniquely created design, and I'm going to help you discover how God wired you to hear Him so you never need to doubt again.

You'll learn to hear God with such confidence that you won't be distracted by what He said to your pastor, your best friend, or the influencers you follow. You'll come to know what hearing God is really about: waking up to who you truly are, embracing your identity as a loved child of God, and living that out every single day.

Once you finally grasp the truth that you are a child of God, something extraordinary happens. You can fully trust that God is speaking to you just as loudly and clearly as He is speaking to every other soul on this planet. You can cultivate that unshakable confidence to attune your ears to His divine voice and fearlessly tread the path He lays before you, knowing that you're loved and valued by the One who created you.

A few of you are still standing on the shore, toeing the water.

I can imagine you thinking, *I don't know, Havilah. Things get dangerous when humans walk around saying God spoke to them. And now you're telling us everyone hears differently? People can't be trusted. They do terrible things in God's name.*

You wouldn't be wrong. People *have* used claims about God's voice to manipulate and abuse others. These behaviors are terrible, heartbreaking, and definitely not of God. But they are nothing to be feared. In chapter 14 I'll talk about how to establish safeguards for yourself and others, safeguards rooted in God's Word and authority. That some people abuse claims about God's voice is no reason to cut yourself off from your one true life-giving source. This is one of the reasons I'm so passionate about teaching this topic.

When you agree that God wants to speak to you and you can hear from Him, you can begin to apply yourself to learning what His voice sounds like. You no longer have to rely on a secondhand experience, hearing God only through others. You can learn how He made *you* to hear—maybe through your ears, but quite possibly with your eyes or your heart or your mind. I'm going to help you figure out which way of hearing is your strongest.

If you're new to the idea that God speaks to individuals, spend some time with me in the following pages. If you would, please approach with an open mind and a willingness to explore a new perspective on God's voice. Do you trust Him to be present in this process? I do. With His help I'm going to demystify some common but misguided beliefs about how He speaks and how people hear. I'm going to show you what's possible through God. Trust me. I believe you're going to experience a real breakthrough.

Come on in. The water's fine!

QUESTIONS WE'RE
EMBARRASSED TO ASK

WHY CAN'T I HEAR GOD?

"When you come looking for me, you'll find me.
Yes, when you get serious about finding me and want it more
than anything else, I'll make sure you won't be disappointed."

–JEREMIAH 29:13–14 MSG

WHEN MY TWIN SISTER AND I WERE KIDS, OUR DAD BURST into the room one day, a glimmer of enthusiasm in his eyes. "Girls, listen up! God spoke to me. He told me about this guy named Paul, sitting on a porch in a blue shirt. We're going on an adventure to find him!"

Full of excitement, Deborah and I hopped into the car. We were going on a treasure hunt for a man wearing a blue shirt!

Dad drove around while Deb and I scanned both sides of the street, noses to the windows, looking for this Paul. I don't remember who first spotted the man sitting on a porch, but it wasn't too long before Dad pulled the car to the curb. Sure enough, the guy was wearing a blue shirt.

Dad climbed out of the car and asked him, "Is your name Paul?"

A hint of wariness appeared in Paul's eyes as he cautiously replied, "Yes, that's me." He stood up to greet us. Without missing a beat, Dad dove right in. "You might find this surprising, but I'm a Christian, and I have conversations with God. And, well, God spoke to me about you. He revealed your name and said I would find you sitting on a porch, wearing blue. God brought me here, Paul, because I believe He wants to intervene in your life."

The man was so shocked he couldn't speak at first. Then, overwhelmed with emotion, Paul began to weep. Trying to get the words out, he admitted he was not a praying man, but he was in desperate need of help. That self-confessed nonpraying man had said a prayer that day, not for a second anticipating that God would answer his prayer by sending my dad to help him.

At this point both men started crying.

My dad asked if he could talk with Paul about God, and the man agreed. As my sister and I looked on, Dad told him the gospel story. "Just like God sent me today to find you," Dad said, "God sent His Son on a mission to Earth to seek and save all those who are lost."

I'll never forget that moment. Right there on the porch, Paul joined my dad in a heartfelt prayer, surrendering his life to Jesus.

That was the environment I grew up in—a place filled with divine encounters. My dad had a prophetic gift and an uncanny ability to discern God's voice, not only for himself but for others as well. It was through him that I first grasped the concept of hearing from God.

It sounds exciting, but it was also intimidating. People who knew my father would often say to me, "Oh, you must hear God too! Are you prophetic?"

They meant it kindly, but honestly, it was really discouraging. Because all I knew for sure was that I was the girl who couldn't hear God's voice.

It wasn't that I couldn't hear *any* voices. In fact, I'm pretty sure I was always hearing at least three: my voice, the enemy's voice, and the voice of God. The problem was, I couldn't figure out which one was which. Who was doing the talking?

That's a pretty big problem. If I asked God a question and an answer came to mind, it would only spark more questions. I'd think, *Wait . . . is that God talking to me? Then I should probably listen. But what if it's the devil and he's trying to tempt me? I should ignore him!* Or even worse, *What if all the chatter is my own self-talk, and the truth is I just need a good night's sleep . . . or therapy?*

Maybe it wouldn't have been so hard if I wasn't constantly surrounded by people who talked *a lot* about God speaking to them. Each story would send me on a journey, and I'd do whatever I could to find the voice of God for myself. I'd zealously buy the book, attend the conference, read the scriptures, join the prayer line, fast for forty days, and lead the prayer meeting. I was the desperate girl wearing the Take My Money T-shirt, and anyone who had anything remotely promising to sell me could have it.

I was constantly trying to get my God channel turned on, but the cable guy never arrived. I couldn't shake the feeling that something was wrong with me.

Why on earth couldn't I hear God clearly? Was He unhappy with my choices? Had I done something to upset Him? I knew I wasn't disqualified from sharing my faith with others and living a life guided by my love for God. But was I willing to accept that I might *never* hear His voice? Was it okay for me to spend yet another year wandering from one conference to another, reading book after book, trying to live my best life without really knowing if it was the life I was meant to live?

Eventually defeated, having tried everything I knew to do, I told myself, "Havilah, your faith in God is enough. You don't need to hear a voice."

That worked for a while, until it didn't.

Inevitably, believers I admired—friends, teachers, leaders, influencers, athletes, movers and shakers, my heroes of the faith—would make some kind of declaration about having heard from God. Over and over, I heard phrases like:

"And that's when God spoke to me."

"That was the moment God told me _____."

"God said I was going to marry that person."

"I saw myself running that business and knew the vision was from God."

The most influential people in my world were hearing God speak to them, and what they heard was changing the trajectory of their lives. It was an undeniable truth: they were guided by divine wisdom, while I felt completely disconnected, spiraling into a pit of spiritual turmoil. The combination of my spiritual anxiety and clichéd phrases like "carpe diem" or "You have only one life, so make it count" created a tumultuous internal storm. I felt like raising my hand to say, "Excuse me! May I ask you a question? Would you please shut up?! You're giving me more anxiety."

WHAT MAKES HEARING GOD SO HARD?

I don't know one human who hasn't woken up in a cold sweat over important decisions that have to be made. "How do I know if I should marry that specific person?" "Should I take that job opportunity? Is it time to move? What about the kids? Is it time to leave or stay? Invest or save?" "What's the best way to handle this relationship problem I'm having?"

And that's just on a Monday.

Then, after we make a choice, we move to obsessing whether it's the right choice. We're in limbo. We feel as if we're in our own little mental purgatory, somewhere between "I have a critical question I need answered" and "Whew . . . I made it to my therapist's office!" It's overwhelming.

We run to church, or better yet, catch an online service, hoping the worship leader or the pastor on the stage will say something to give us our much-needed answer. Or at least something to ease the nagging anxiety that we're messing up everything. Maybe we'll find the missing corner piece to our life's puzzle. Someone might hand us the answer we desperately need.

It isn't often that going to church stops the questions from bouncing around in our heads.

How do I know if it's God speaking to me?

What if it's the devil tormenting me?

What if I'm getting in my own way by just thinking what I want to hear and then slapping a God sticker on it?

We buy the journals labeled "Goal Chasers" or "Dream Bigger." We repost meaningful quotes to exude a sense of confidence that uncertainty is normal. We mimic others who seem to know what God is saying, people who look like they have it all together. We buy the books, attend the retreats, read the Bible, and consume a ton of information but never find that core confidence that we *can* and *do* hear God.

With all the available help, why aren't we more certain about our sense of things?

7

A lack of devotion to God is usually not the problem. At the time of my own crisis, I was wholly committed to God. This was not a problem of spiritual apathy. What fascinates me when I look back on this thread in my life is that my commitment began with a surreal confidence that I *had* heard the voice of God!

A lack of devotion to God is usually not the problem.

When I was seventeen years old, I had a life-altering moment.

The night started like any other night. Some guys had picked up my sister and me, and we were headed to a party. But in the darkness of that car, in the nauseating normal, something life-changing happened.

I sensed something shifting in the car. I now know it was the Holy Spirit. I began to hear God speaking to me in my heart.

He said, *Havilah, what are you doing? I've called you to more than living for the weekend. You cannot live like this anymore. You have a destiny and a calling. You've got to be courageous! Fight for your life! Get out of here!*

He had my full attention. As my mind began to race, time seemed to stand still and my heart beat wildly. I felt I couldn't be silent any longer. I asked the guys to turn down the music so I could speak. I blurted out, "I have a call of God on my life!"

I wish I could convey how utterly awkward this moment was. There was no piano player or pastor in the background. No one nodding in affirmation as I made this proclamation. Quite the opposite. An uncomfortable silence filled the car, and the dark silhouettes of the two guys in the front seat didn't move. Nothing about it felt spiritual. And yet I was confident God had spoken to me.

Spoiler alert: I didn't go to the party, and I've been serving God ever since.[1]

Even though that encounter with God profoundly changed my life, it didn't spare me from confusion about what it means to hear from God. How could that young woman also be the one who couldn't distinguish God's voice from racing thoughts or a bad night's sleep? From that day on I jumped into the deep end of my faith, staying busy with our church by volunteering, serving, and learning. I was doing my best to grow and develop my life.

But when the noise of each day faded and I was left alone with my thoughts, a deep longing settled into my soul. I knew there *must* be a way to access more of God. If He could tap me on the shoulder and say, *Follow Me,* then surely I could ask Him for guidance, right? Couldn't I also tap *Him* on the shoulder and ask Him anything at any time . . . and expect to get an answer? There had to be a way to stay in that miraculous secret space where I had heard God.

Even if we're 100 percent certain we've heard God speak to us at some point in our lives, our lack of confidence is a common problem. Why?

We all have our theories. For years I thought my learning disabilities were to blame. In the third grade I was diagnosed with dyslexia with reading and comprehension issues. Dyslexia is a neurological condition that makes it hard to process written words. I figured my issues might extend to understanding spoken words as well. I also got a diagnosis of attention-deficit/hyperactivity disorder (ADHD), which can make it hard to focus for any length of time. Maybe I simply couldn't pay attention when God was talking to me. My sunny personality and sociability covered up this deep dark fear.

When I was fifteen, my sister and I joined a six-week summer program with a nonprofit called Youth with a Mission (YWAM). The trip included **learning presentations** to perform up and down the midwestern states. Each morning after breakfast and before rehearsal, the staff sent all fifty of us kids off to our own private corners for a quiet time. Simply put, we would take personal time to invite God to speak to us. Bibles encouraged. Journals required.

I hated it.

I'd wander someplace no one else had discovered, only to sit there killing time for an hour. I didn't know how to hear God speak to me, so I didn't know what I was supposed to do. I had a deep ache for connection with Him. I had plenty of nagging, life-impacting questions, not the least of which was, *What did You create me to do, God?* But day after day I heard nothing but silence. I tried to read, I overshared in prayer, and eventually I wrote something down.

Two decades later, I picked up the journal from that summer. The first thing I read on the front page was, "God if You're there, I can't hear You."

Page two: "God, what are You saying to me?"

On another page: "Where are You?"

A few more pages had similar phrases.

The rest of the journal was blank.

As an adult with twenty years of wisdom under my belt, I held that journal in my hands and felt empathy for my younger self. I was able to see the truth for the first time: My struggle wasn't about my learning issues. It wasn't about my ADHD or that I didn't have an iPhone back then to read the Bible aloud to me. I wasn't lacking a spiritual mind-set or a pure heart. God wasn't waiting for me to get it together so I could be somehow holy enough to hear Him.

Are you ready for this?

Not hearing God speak to me was a universal problem I'd tragically interpreted as a personal problem. I wasn't alone in the struggle.

REASON #1: WE THINK THERE'S ONLY ONE WAY TO HEAR

Most of us are taught that hearing God's voice just happens. Listen hard enough and you will hear. God will come to you. We learn this from our parents or our pastors, small group leaders, spiritual mentors, and the church at large. "You'll know God's voice when you hear it," we're told. "All you need to do is ask . . . and ask . . . and ask again . . . you know . . . until your supernatural radio station comes in clearly. Add it to your list of saved stations and voilà! You now hear God!"

After all this, if you muster up the courage to admit you *still* can't hear God, that's when people in the know will go to the default answer: "Just read your Bible; that's how God speaks to you." Of course, the Bible is God's Word, and His printed words speak to us and help us. But deep down we know it's not enough to read the messages someone sends us when what we really want is to spend time in the same room with them. Knowing someone loves you is not the same as experiencing their love firsthand.

I, too, was taught all these things. This is nobody's fault. After all, that's exactly how it works for some people. "Read more, pray more, listen harder, listen better," makes perfect sense if it aligns with the way you are made. If not, you're out of luck.

Maybe you're naturally curious and willing to ask others when or how they hear God. This can be helpful—unless the story of their hearing is all about a lightning-bolt-from-heaven moment, confirming you're still basically in the dark, waiting to be struck yourself.

If you're part of the failed-results group, you might find yourself stuck in years of painful, pleading prayers, discouragement, and deep soul fatigue called *hopelessness*. You might give up. You might park yourself in the shadow of a spiritual person who hears God for you. Or worse, you might resign yourself to faking it. I was usually in the fake-it-till-you-make-it camp, which seemed pretty lonely even though I wasn't the only one there.

In this lonely space it's easy for us to latch onto that false belief that everyone but you can hear God. Everyone but you knows the secret handshake. Here we draw dangerous conclusions: God is exclusive. He has favorites. There are only so many seats at the table, and they have all been taken. There is no space for you.

Tragically, this is where most of us disengage.

But I want to applaud you for being here, right now, reading this book. That means you haven't disengaged yet, and I'm thrilled about that. In the second and third sections of this book, we're going to get to all the ways in which God speaks to and through each of His children, including you.

REASON #2: WE HAVE OVERCOMPLICATED GOD

You're too spiritual. Yes, that's what I said. Your idyllic concept of spirituality as something separate from your day-to-day life is keeping you from hearing God spiritually *in* your day-to-day life.

Let me explain by asking you a question: What is spiritual?

Hmm, let's see. Going to church, praying, giving to the poor, helping the needy, worshiping, fasting, serving others—anything that involves an experience of God in a situation where we expect God to show up.

Okay, next question: What is unspiritual or secular?

You might list things like going to work, shopping for groceries, taking care of the kids, weeding the yard, taking vacations—ordinary, day-to-day events that don't involve an experience of God.

But do you honestly believe that God can't or won't be involved in the most mundane aspects of your life? Oddly, the ideology that some things are spiritual and other things are secular is everywhere in the church but hard to find in the Bible. Pastor John Mark Comer writes:

Look up the word "spiritual" in Genesis to Malachi—the Bible used by Jesus. It's not there. Why? Because in a Hebrew worldview, all of life is spiritual. Even when you get to the New Testament, the word spiritual is really only used by Paul. In his writings, it means "animated by the Holy Spirit." And for Paul, every facet of our lives should be spiritual. I think if you had asked Jesus about His spiritual life, He would have looked at you very confused. My guess is He would have asked, "What do you mean by My spiritual life? All of My life is spiritual." Jesus didn't buy into sacred/secular thinking. To Him, life is a seamless, integrated, holistic experience where the sacred is all around us. And because everything is spiritual, everything matters to God.[2]

Even so, some of us can't avoid that some things just feel more spiritual and other things feel more secular. This is important because too many of us think that people who hear God are super-spiritual, and to hear God we must become *more* spiritual. This isn't true. *Spiritual* isn't something that you have to become; it's something that you already are in Christ. Just because somebody has a certain kind of spiritual gift—say,

Too many of us think that people who hear God are super-spiritual, and to hear God we must become *more* spiritual. This isn't true.

prophecy—doesn't mean your gifts, your ability to hear God, or anything you bring to the table aren't also profoundly spiritual in their own way.

We do contribute, my friends, not just as a mere habit but as a powerful tool to step fully into our identity in Christ. You see, it's not just about us; it's about blessing God and the people He places in our path. And here's the beautiful thing: we can do this in the most ordinary of situations.

It's amazing how often we stand in our own way when it comes to thinking we can't hear God. (We all do it—nothing to feel bad about.) But another thing that stands between us and God is simple ignorance. No one has ever explained why hearing God is important in the first place. In the next chapter, I'm going to do just that.

DOES IT MATTER IF I HEAR GOD OR NOT?

Whether you turn to the right or to the left, your ears will hear a voice behind you, saying, "This is the way; walk in it."

−ISAIAH 30:21

MANY OF US HAVE EXPERIENCED TRAUMA. WE'VE BEEN frozen in those moments where the world seems to stop, and we don't know if we're going to make it to the next breath. We've lost jobs, we've lost loved ones, we've lost property and health. In these times I think about God's voice, and I realize how much I value it, the constant reminder that He is with me.

One morning I heard the kind of scream a parent's heart knows is bad. I have four sons. Our home is wild, and there's lots of energy. When the boys were little there was lots of crying too. Sometimes a mom hears an upset child and thinks, *Yeah, you're being dramatic, but you're going to live.* This was not that kind of sound.

It came from our third-born, Grayson. I found our eighteen-month-old outside, terrified, pounding on our sliding glass doors. Blood was coming out of his mouth and was running down his shirt. I was stunned. He had broken a screen in a window on the second story of our home and fallen onto a concrete slab.

A blur of emergency calls, an ambulance ride, and an ER visit ensued. At the hospital we were ushered into the same room we were in a year earlier when Grayson nearly drowned. (If you ever wonder why I look tired or broke, there you go.) I didn't know how serious his injuries might be, because the people who could tell me were busy doing their jobs. Someone said he might have internal bleeding. We rushed to radiology for a scan.

"Okay, Mom," the technician said. "I need two things from you." I was relieved to finally be able to do something to help. "I need you to hold Grayson's head steady, because he needs to be as still as possible. Also, I need you to talk to him by leaning over him. Speak words that will keep him awake and calm. Say his name and tell him he's going to be okay."

I'll never forget that moment. I leaned over Grayson with no idea of what would happen while fear frantically knocked on the door of my heart. I didn't know if we were going to lose him. I did my best to steady my trembling hands as I held his head, and I looked into his eyes while speaking to him softly, constantly. "I love you, Grayson. Mommy loves you. I love you so much. You're going to be okay. It's okay, Grayson. We're helping you. That man over there is helping us." Terror was all over Grayson's face.

He went into the machine, came back out. Went in, came out. Time seemed to stand still.

As I was leaning over Grayson, holding his head, and comforting him, I felt the Holy Spirit lean over my life and say, *Whatever happens, Havilah, you're going to make it. You're going to be okay. I've got you. I'm here to help you.*

The third time Grayson came out of the scanner, I felt him take a deep breath. Then all the color rushed back into his face. He looked at me with his little blue eyes, and I saw the spark come back into them. He gave me a smile.

When it was over the technician came to retrieve us, leading us to the exit. I quickly grabbed his arm, ignoring appropriate boundaries, and asked him, "Is it really bad? Please, can you tell me anything?"

Seeing my desperation, he said, "Well, I can't tell you anything, but if it helps, if it were really bad, you'd have a nurse with you."

I heaved a sigh of relief. When a nurse came in to take us back to the room, for a hot second I thought about yelling, "Get out of here! Get out in the name of Jesus!"

Miraculously, Grayson wasn't seriously injured. During his fall, he had cut only his tongue. That's where the blood was coming from. Other than a few bumps and bruises, he was fine. The doctor gave us the good news and said, "All is well, Grayson is okay, and you can leave now."

I stood there shocked. You can only imagine the extreme lows and highs we'd felt in just a few hours. I said to the doctor, "Well, my family can leave but I'm staying. I'll need a bed and some drugs please, and like right now!"

I tend to make jokes in intense situations. Everyone laughed and I went out with my family. After leaving the ER, I stood in the parking lot hugging my husband, Ben, with Grayson squeezed between us while happy tears streamed down our faces onto his little body. We hugged. Prayed. Thanked God for another day with our son.

When we are in crisis, God leans over us and speaks words of comfort in the same way any loving parent would do for their panicked child. If we can hear Him, we can hear His love in that voice of comfort when we need comfort, that voice of connection when we need connection, that voice of guidance when we need guidance.

The Holy Spirit speaks this way over us in every environment that we enter. When our world feels chaotic and we don't have answers to our questions and we don't know what to do, the Holy Spirit wants to grab us, look us in the eyes, and say, *I am not hiding from you, sweetheart. I'm not hiding from you, My son. I got you. I'm going to speak the words you need to keep you alive in this season.*

His is the voice above all other voices that has the power to settle us. It's what saves us from having to be the biggest person in the room—the intellectual, the emotionally intelligent, the one who has the right answer to every question. Instead, we can be the one who relies on the God who knows us and created us and formed us, the God who can speak to the storm.

His is the voice that says, *I know you, I see you, I love you, I'm with you.* Our lives are extremely important to Him, and He has real opinions about every detail, even about those things we think aren't valuable enough to bring to Him. *Nothing is too much to ask of Me,* He says. *Let Me be God. I'm really, really good at it.* When we recognize that voice, we experience its power. We can rest in its protection. Everything changes, even if it seems like nothing changes. The gift that we have in hearing God's voice is one of the greatest gifts that we've been given and will get us through any moment of crisis.

Hearing God's voice is the thing that will get us through in moments of crisis.

THE POWER OF A CONNECTED LIFE

When we disconnect from the Divine, we go from thriving to surviving. We're reduced to grabbing scraps off the floor instead of pulling up a seat to the table loaded with God's feast. When we're in survival mode, we make terrible decisions. We waste opportunities. Our lives become fear-based rather than faith-based.

Let me ask you a few critical questions:

- How can you have a relationship with God if you can't hear Him?
- How can you live as you were created without ever speaking to your Creator?
- How can you access all His resources if your conversation isn't a two-way street?

Every single day we face a crazy number of situations that require our response. If we don't know how to hear God's voice, we have to react to all those things on our own. Blindly. No wonder we deal with so much collective anxiety and depression.

But God, who doesn't force Himself on anyone, would like to step fully into your life and show you what is possible. It's hard for Him to do that if you can't hear everything He's trying to say.

The human need for connection is undeniable. An unmet need for connection and communication is deadly.[1] The hopelessness will kill you. I am not being melodramatic.

According to psychologist Amy Sullivan, your level of cortisol, a stress hormone, goes up when you're lonely. Chronic stress can lead to many health issues, including heart disease and cancer. Because of its many health risks, recent studies compare the effects of loneliness to smoking fifteen cigarettes a day.[2]

19

Additionally, studies show having a relationship with God and hearing Him speak to you has enormous value. Numerous studies show that people who report feeling God's love directly feel less lonely, less anxious, less fearful, and less stressed.[3] Connection to God is vital for your whole self—mind, body, soul, and spirit. The bottom line: hearing God speak to you is good for you, but *not* hearing God speak is stressful and potentially dangerous. Why? Because intimate connection with your Creator is a need, not a want.

Wants are desires. They can be dismissed. Ignored. Outgrown. Your wants change depending on the season, your age, your circumstances, and so on. Wants come and go. They are useful but not essential.

Needs are essential. They cannot be dismissed. They stay until they get met. Period. Your needs demand to be met—it's your choice whether that happens in healthy or unhealthy ways—and if you don't meet your needs, you will die or feel dead. Ignoring our needs is no way to live. In fact, it's unsustainable.

If you get only one thing out of this book, here it is:

Hearing God speak isn't a want. It's a serious and vital need. It's essential to emotional and spiritual health. The nagging ache you sometimes feel cannot be relieved except by divine connection. You can try to ignore your need to hear from God, but at your core you and every human on earth have a need to be known. When you feel known, you are safe to belong. When you feel known, you feel loved. The power of being known is enormous.

Jesus talked about this exact thing: "I am the vine, and you are the branches. If you stay joined to me, and I to you, you will produce plenty of fruit. But separated from me you won't be able to do anything" (John 15:5 ERV).

The truth is undeniable: we were created for connection. The best part? You don't *have* to do life alone! Because you are a branch joined to the vine of Christ, you have an all-access pass to God. When you live connected to God, you live connected to your power source. You live a powerful life because you have a powerful God. You have access to the miraculous!

When you live connected to God, you have access to the miraculous!

Just as a lamp needs to be plugged in, your life needs to be connected to your power source. If a lamp isn't working, you don't start yelling at it, telling it to try harder. You don't sit there wondering if it's defective. That's just crazy! A lamp wasn't created to light up on its own. It must be plugged into its power source, and when it's connected, it works as designed.

To put it another way: if you live a life disconnected from God, you are disconnected from all the resources available through Him. Without a God connection, life is infinitely harder than necessary. Maybe even unbearable. Sure, you'll live out your own success story. Maybe you get the degree and marry your high school sweetheart. You can have the kid, buy the house, and make a brand out of yourself. But apart from God, it will never be enough.

WHY SETTLE FOR A SECOND-RATE EXISTENCE?

In his gospel, John told the story of a woman who came to get water from a well in the middle of the day. Jesus struck up a conversation with her. It took a shocking turn when He asked her to get Him some water.

The woman answered, "I am surprised that you ask me for a drink! You are a Jew and I am a Samaritan woman!" (Jews have nothing to do with Samaritans.)

Jesus answered, "You don't know what God can give you. And you don't know who I am, the one who asked you for a drink. If you knew, you would have asked me, and I would have given you living water."

The woman said, "Sir, where will you get that living water? The well is very deep, and you have nothing to get water with. Are you greater than our ancestor Jacob? He is the one who gave us this well. He drank from it himself, and his sons and all his animals drank from it too."

Jesus answered, "Everyone who drinks this water will be thirsty again. But anyone who drinks the water I give will never be thirsty again. The water I give people will be like a spring flowing inside them. It will bring them eternal life." (John 4:9–14 ERV)

The woman was thinking only of an external connection to meet her needs. She wasn't wrong. But Jesus was saying she needed more.

When you landed on this round planet, you were as cute as you were needy. You came with a set of visible needs, and those needs were basic: food, warmth, clothing, shelter, protection. But you had invisible needs too. Things like comfort, belonging, love, compassion, and empathy.

Jesus was revealing to this woman that she had needs outside of the daily grind. He showed her a glimpse of the *supernatural* available in her *natural*. Think about it: She was not in a synagogue, a church, or a temple. She was getting water, doing what needed to be done, and Jesus interrupted her daily life to speak to her. He explained that He knew a way to meet her deepest needs—not just daily water for the body but also divine nourishment for the soul, which has a thirst that can be quenched only through connection and communication with God.

As I've said, connection to our Creator is vital for our mental, emotional, physical, and spiritual health. God wants to be an endless source and resource for us. And yet most of us (yes, I'm talking about Jesus-loving people) are living disconnected from the Divine, trying to figure out life on our own.

If we're disconnected and desperate, we'll try to use someone else's connection to God for ourselves. There's nothing wrong with asking a trusted friend or mentor for wisdom or accepting a word from God delivered by another person, but God never intended for us to wait for others to connect us to heaven. Why settle for second-hand knowledge, leftovers, or a limited human supply?

Think about the difference between a reservoir and a well. They look the same. Both hold water, and both can quench your thirst for a time. But a reservoir holds water someone puts into it, and a well provides water from a greater source and doesn't need to be replenished. Any human you turn to, no matter how easily they hear God, is offering you water from their own limited reservoir. They can't offer you water from the bottomless well you could get directly from God.

Too many of us are willing to settle for water from a reservoir when we could be living on water from the bottomless well of divine connection. We live like this until *we wake up and understand the power of a connected life*, which is the purpose of this book.

Now more than ever before I hear people saying they are finished with trying to "be a Christian." They dismiss the spiritual awakening that brought them to Christ. They deem organized religion an outdated if not outright villainous institution. They refer to their brothers and sisters in Christ as "those people," as if to blame others for shutting them out. Why?

So many of them have said to me, with varying levels of discouragement or desperation, "I can't hear God." Here's the thing: I believe them. They've been living a second-class spiritual experience that would tempt anyone to want to give up.

If any of the struggles I've described in this chapter resonate with you, I invite you to reflect on a few questions.

- Could my struggles with anxiety, pain, frustration, and apathy have the same cause?
- Am I struggling because I'm not plugged in to God?
- Could the ache deep inside me exist because of an invisible disconnection?
- Could my disconnection be leading me to think things that are untrue, or to do things I don't want to do?

I'm convinced that learning how to stay connected to God is just as important as having electricity in your home. Imagine what your life could be like if your purpose had an endless supply of power. What if you could know the answers to your questions anytime, anywhere? Now imagine having none of that. (Some of us don't have to think too hard.) Living as a person of faith without being connected will cost you more than your electricity bill. And learning to connect with God will change your whole life. It certainly changed mine.

THE RIPPLE EFFECT OF CONNECTION

In chapter 1 I described my struggles with feeling like a second-class Christian because I didn't hear God the way others did. Somewhere along the way I began to open myself up to radical possibilities.

- Maybe I'm not a failure or a heathen—I'm just trying to ignore my insatiable need for connection.
- What if my negative choices are nothing more than a weak effort to have my way or to get through another day?
- Could my discouragement be caused by disconnection, and is that what's making me feel defeated?

I'm happy to report God met me in answering these questions and began to teach me the truth. Since then, the insights He has given me have opened doors to teach thousands of people throughout North and South America, Europe, and Australia. I've had a front-row seat to thousands of people learning to hear the voice of God immediately and continuously.

People who are connected to God are powerful conductors of supernatural electricity. When we are connected to God, He can use our connection to help and serve others. The ripple effect is profound. Together, all of us who are connected have the potential to change thousands of lives. And there has never been a more crucial time to strengthen our connection.

Once you learn how to hear God's voice, it becomes the anchor that stabilizes every aspect of your life. You can apply His words again and again as He leads you into the life He purposed for you to live. It's the grounding force that distinguishes those of us who *hear and know* from those of us who are *still searching*.

Sometimes in our spiritual walk we forget the gifts we've received. I think the enemy works hard to make us forget our full ability to live the life God wants for us. But when Jesus left the earth, He said (and this is my paraphrase), "I am not leaving you without anything. I'm giving you a gift. I'll be up standing at the right hand of the Father interceding on your behalf, but you are not going to lack a thing. The Holy Spirit is going to be with you all the way through" (John 14).

The Holy Spirit in our lives, the Spirit that speaks to us, is a gift of connection. It's not something we have to earn. It's one of the greatest gifts of our salvation. It's one of the greatest gifts that we can share with others, for it is how we all can draw near to Him. When we receive this gift of God's presence, we become partners with Him, which empowers us to live fully present to our purpose on the planet.

WHAT CAN I DO DIFFERENTLY?

"Forget the former things;
do not dwell on the past.
See, I am doing a new thing!
Now it springs up; do you not perceive it?"

—ISAIAH 43:18–19

WHEN I WAS SEVENTEEN AND NOT AT ALL SURE HOW to hear from God despite my Follow-Me experience, my sister and I attended a weeklong church conference in Southern California. On the first night a guy approached Deb and said, "God told me you have a word for me. Would you pray for me?"

Her first thought was, *Is this a pickup line? Is this what people do in church to hit on each other?* Outside of church, a person might say, "You're cute." But inside the church, it's better to ask, "Will you pray for me? Better yet . . . lay hands on me?"

I digress.

As the problem-solving twin, I instructed Deb to ignore him at all costs. Clearly, this was a weird request from a stranger.

My sister didn't want to encourage him, so when he approached her a second time, she said, "I'll pray for you later." (This is how Christians often get out of things. We say things like, "Well, when the Lord leads," or "God said no." You know I'm right!)

Throughout the week this guy continued to repeatedly ask Deb if she would pray for him. She avoided him and hoped he'd forget. Then, after midnight on the final night, after receiving prayer, the two of us got up to leave. Deb felt a tap on her shoulder, and when she turned around he was standing right in front of her.

"It's the last night. Can you pray for me now?" he asked.

My sister and I made eye contact with each other as if to say, *Dang, no more excuses.* Add in that we were—and still are— recovering pastor's kids who didn't know how to live without a main course of obligation and a side of guilt, and Deb grudgingly agreed.

She wrangled me and our prophetically gifted friend Staci to help, and we three gathered around him. Deb and I, using our twin senses, had an unspoken agreement that we would pray a short prayer. After placing our hands on his shoulders, we began to pray.

I remember feeling so aggravated. Standing there I thought, *I don't want to pray for this guy. I don't even know him, and I don't know how to hear God's voice. This is so dumb.*

It got worse. You know that sensation you get when you're in an awkward situation, already feeling intimidated, then someone puts you on the spot? So you feel even more intimidated, but now you're angry too? Everything inside wants to get the heck out of there because you're in way over your head. Yes? Okay, so you're tracking.

Picture this: we're standing there with our eyes closed, praying for this desperate dude, the guy who can't take a hint and keeps invading our personal space, and Staci says, "Havilah, I think you have a word for him."

My eyes popped open. I looked straight at her, hoping to make eye contact, but her eyes were closed. I panicked, thinking, *Staci, I'm going to punch you. I don't have a word, and now you're calling me out. You seriously have the nerve to say my name?*

My thoughts kicked into overdrive. *I'm dead. Humiliated. Overwhelmed.* Then a rational thought appeared. Staci knew I had a twin. She could have easily said, "One of you has a word," but instead she called *me* out. By name! Which could only mean . . .

I froze in full terror.

My fake-it-till-you-make-it days were over. There are a few things a person can fake, but I knew that hearing from God shouldn't be one of them. God would speak to me or He wouldn't. As I looked at Staci, she said—her eyes closed the whole time—"Havilah, just close your eyes and say the first thing that comes to you."

I closed my eyes. It was 1:00 a.m., and the first thing that popped into my mind was McDonald's fries! Because, well, I was a teenager and I was hungry.

I thought, *That can't be God*, because I was young but not dumb. So I closed my eyes again, trying to ignore the fries.

Everyone waited for me, sitting in this awkward silence. Then suddenly in my mind's eye the name Meshach appeared.

I knew the guy's name wasn't Meshach, and that sent my head spinning. *What does this mean? This is crazy. What if it's wrong?*

But my inner rage over being forced to pray for this guy, and the humiliation of being called out by name, motivated me to just say it. I admit thinking if it was wrong, maybe the guy kind of deserved it. Not my greatest moment.

I opened my eyes and said, "I don't know if this means anything to you, but I got the name Meshach."

In an instant the guy dropped to the ground and started sobbing. I don't know which of us was more shocked. I didn't know what was happening, but I thought it might be good? Clearly the name meant something profound to him. My sister and Staci shared a few more things with him. Their words also had a clear impact. Maybe he was the emotional type.

When we finished, he picked himself up off the floor and walked away with puffy eyes, a tear-stained shirt, and a huge smile. He was clearly connected to his Creator in ways we would never know.

Deeply relieved, Deb and I gathered our things to leave. Then, lo and behold, the guy came back! With a friend! The question was all over his face: Could we pray for him too?

I was thinking, *No, absolutely not. I will not. Listen, I just got through praying for you, remember? We just—*

Before I could say anything, Staci quickly agreed. What could I do but surrender? I was in way over my head anyway. Again, in the middle of the prayer, Staci blurted out, "I think you have something for him, Havilah."

Could she be serious? I was so done with her calling me out publicly. I had a twin sister standing right next to me. Why didn't Staci call *her* out?

Knowing I had nothing to lose, I bowed my head again. Listened. Another name rose to the surface: Shadrach. Privately I said to God, *No offense, but You have a huge Bible to pick from. Did You mean to go to the same story?*[1] Then I wondered, *Do I have the gift of names? What's up with the names?*

So I just said, "I feel like God is saying 'Shadrach' over you." You guessed it: the guy fell to the ground and started weeping, just like his friend. I was stunned. I didn't know what was going on, but something was happening. Something supernatural.

A line had started to form. More people wanted prayer. I just flowed with it. As we prayed, I listened, but this time I knew what I was waiting for. I knew how God would present His voice to me.

The next guy came, and we prayed for him. Another name, another cryfest, another invisible connection between God and me and these guys. It happened *four times*. When we finished, the four of them stood and put their arms around each other, a band of brothers.

I will never forget that moment. All four of them faced us, their faces puffy from weeping, and one of them finally explained: "A prophet came to our church last summer, and he singled out each one of us. We weren't seated together. He began to prophesy over us, saying, 'You're a Meshach. You're a Shadrach, you're an Abednego, and you're a Daniel.'" The names God had given to me for each of these guys confirmed the prophecy they had received months earlier.

"We're sure you hear this all the time," one said to me, "but that was an extraordinary prophetic word."

Seriously. What is this life?

EMBRACE THE UNEXPECTED

It was a completely mind-boggling experience. Maybe if Meshach and his friends had known they were in amateur hour, they'd have been less enthusiastic. But our cool seventeen-year-old selves weren't going to give that away, quickly responding yes! In a euphoric state, we walked out to our car on a complete high.

My mind raced through all my senses. I was stunned. I had heard the voice of God again! But not in the way I had anticipated.

All those altar calls I'd responded to, books I'd read, prayers I'd prayed, people I'd imitated—none of that had prepared me for what I'd actually experienced. I had imagined that hearing God would feel so much more spiritual than it did. I'd anticipated an audible voice speaking to me, or a vision, maybe even an angelic visitation—an undeniable force as powerful as the one I'd heard in the car, inviting me to follow Him. Maybe God would even take control of my body and speak through my mouth!

I was dead wrong.

I didn't have a major encounter with God. I had a small, clear thought, a mere impression, really, that grew just big enough for me to notice it. And when I did, I wasn't confident at first that the impression was really from Him. That confidence came later, from familiarity forged over the years. Today, I *know* it was Him. Nothing can make me question that.

The whole event was something like a dreamy first kiss. Afterward, you wonder, *Did that really happen? Oh my gosh—it really did! I know what it feels like now. Wow! That was easier than I thought. I want to do it again!*

Here's a fact: whatever success I've had in hearing God's voice came from a slow-burning, gradual discovery, not a clap-of-thunder supernatural awakening. I'll talk about this more in chapter 7.

I slowly began to recognize the means God used to speak to me. I realized I had been so consumed with discovering *what God was saying* that I had never stopped to consider *how I was designed to hear Him*. As the years passed, I grew in my perception of His voice. He had a lot to say to me, not just about those big critical moments but also about little life decisions. I began hearing His voice speaking to me about reaching more people. I started sharing messages from God with a few individuals, which gradually grew into many, then hundreds, and eventually thousands of people.

When I grew strong in my hearing, God led me to start teaching others how to hear Him. I have done this for decades now. Through my interactions with others, I realized that the mistake I made on a personal level is the same mistake we have made on a collective level: we don't understand that people hear God differently, in ways uniquely tailored just for them.

Before we begin to unpack this truth, I want to be fully transparent with you. I'm not a clever person. I'm the girl who wants to know the bare minimum so I can slip by. Sometimes my internal narrative sounds like, *Just give me the bottom line—and* quickly, *so I can look spiritual and smart too!* I've used the phrase "fake it till you make it" an embarrassing number of times.

I'm not a researcher. Or a theologian. Or even an avid reader. I barely graduated high school, and in full disclosure, I was home-schooled my senior year so only my mom knows if I finished and I've asked her to take the truth to her grave.

But my experience with thousands of people has led me to believe this with all my heart, and it has yet to be challenged: God doesn't speak in the same way to everyone. This has fascinated me and compelled me to dive deeper. Over time I identified four specific methods that God uses to communicate with us. I call these methods Prophetic Personalities, and they are personalized filters through which each of us can uniquely listen to God speak.

PROPHETIC: How *God* shows up in your world
PERSONALITY: How *you* show up in your world

We hear God best where these two things meet. Your Prophetic Personality is simply the way God designed you to develop an intimate relationship with Him. Think of it as your spiritual "love language,"[2] which God uses to affirm His deep love for you. God designed you this way so that He and you can easily communicate. What I discovered helped people understand how to hear His voice personally and immediately. Over and over as I taught, I heard success stories from individuals who went from hearing nothing to hearing daily. None of these people needed to attend the right Bible college or pass a special test. It was working!

Now I want to help you too.

If you want to hear God's voice, here's the first thing I'm going to ask you to do: be willing to let go of any misconceived religious dogma or misguided expectations or false beliefs that are keeping you stuck. For example, "Listening to God is super hard," or "If God doesn't speak to me the way He speaks to my friend Cole, it can't be God." You've got to let go of any idealized visions you have of the way God speaks and the way people hear. Every exchange is personal. If you can let go of these limiting beliefs, you can begin to see how God's voice shows up in your life and finally experience its true power. And here's the thing: your life really does depend on it.

Are you ready to take the leap?

ANCHOR THESE CORE BELIEFS IN YOUR HEART AND MIND

If you want to hear God immediately and consistently, you need to understand a few essential truths. These aren't my thoughts; they can easily be found in your Bible.

What is our God-given purpose on this earth? To be known by God (John 10:14), to know Him (Matt. 6:33; Prov. 3:5–6), and to make Him known (Matt. 24:14; Mark 16:15).

New Testament scholar Brian Rosner calls being known by God the "Cinderella of Theology."[3] We bring nothing from the cinders of our lives to the table with God. We have no pedigree that makes us worthy of Him. If you aren't ready to believe His divine love exists or applies to you, I would like to challenge you to continue reading and keep your heart open to the possibility.

Keeping this three-pronged purpose in mind—to be known by God, to know Him, and to make Him known—I'm going to share three life-changing truths that I want you to understand and apply to your life. If you adopt them as part of your mind-set, your life *will* begin to change. I promise.

1. You are a spiritual being.

To be a spiritual being means that we have a nonphysical aspect to our existence that connects us to God and the spiritual realm.

One day while reading 1 Thessalonians, God gave me a revelation that has really helped me understand how I was made: "May God himself, the God of peace, sanctify you through and through. May your whole spirit, soul and body be kept blameless at the coming of our Lord Jesus Christ" (5:23).

In the passage I understood Paul to be making a clear distinction between our spirit, soul, and body, implying that human beings are triune beings. Our Creator designed us this way, with three parts that make up who we are.

Sound complicated? Here's how I've learned to break it down.

Our body is the physical vessel that carries us through life. It is the tangible, visible part of us that interacts with the world around us. Our soul, on the other hand, includes our mind, will, and emotions. It is the seat of our personality, the place where our thoughts and feelings reside. Our spirit is the deepest part of us, the part that connects us to God. It is where God lives if invited.

While we can't separate these three parts of ourselves, we can identify them and understand how they work together. Our soul and spirit are housed within our physical body, and they interact with one another in complex ways. For example, our God-given emotions can influence our very human thoughts, which in turn can impact our physical, earthly body.

Understanding this triune nature of our being has been incredibly helpful for me. It has helped me make sense of my world and what God is doing in my life. I recognize that there are other ways to view our nature, but this simplified model has helped me make sense of things.

The key takeaway from this understanding is that our spirit is dead unless it is awakened. Just like a hand fits inside a glove, so God's Spirit fits inside our spirit. Our spirit was made to fully contain God—and only God! When we invite God into our lives, our spirit comes alive. We become more fully who we were created to be, and we begin to experience the abundant life that Jesus promised us.

Picture it this way: like a deflated balloon, you live with a spirit that was created to be filled. The only way to live with a fully alive (inflated) spirit is to ask the Holy Spirit to come live inside you.

Our very existence comes from God. According to the Bible, God breathed life into Adam, and we are all descended from him. This means that we are all imbued with the breath of God, the same breath that gave us life. In ancient Greek, the original language of the New Testament, the word *pneuma* (πνεῦμα) carries a range of meanings, including life, force, energy, dynamism, and power. "The

Jews considered pneuma to be the powerful force put forth by God to create the universe and all living things and also the force that continues to sustain creation."[4] You know this word—we use it in English related to breath. Pneumonia. Pneumatic. Pneumatologist.

In the New Testament, the Greek word *pneuma* is used to describe the Holy Spirit, which is the same breath of God that awakens us to a spiritual life. Recognizing that our existence comes from God and that we are imbued with His breath has many implications for our lives.

In John 14:26, Jesus explained to the disciples that He would soon send the Holy Spirit to act on His behalf and in His place. Now, instead of having God walking beside us in the flesh, we have God living within us.

Having an alive spirit is truly life-changing! When God comes into the room, every good thing He has for you—hope, healing, vision, a new mind, a new heart—comes with Him. These benefits are made possible by His Spirit, which is the source of everything we desire. The best part is that having an alive spirit grants us access to the supernatural!

When God comes into the room, every good thing He has for you comes with Him.

This means that we can experience the fullness of God's power in our lives. We can overcome challenges, live with purpose, and fulfill our God-given destiny. It reminds us of our connection to God and our dependence on Him for our very existence. It also reminds us that we were created for a purpose, to be in relationship with God and to live a spiritual life.

I want to encourage you to invite the breath of God, the Holy Spirit, to fill your spirit. When we invite the Holy Spirit into our lives, we are inviting God's presence and power to work within us, transforming us from the inside out. This allows us to live a life that is pleasing to God and deeply fulfilling to us.

2. You were created to know His voice.

The book of John talks about knowing God's voice using a metaphor of God as shepherd. "When he [the Good Shepherd] has brought out all his own, he goes on ahead of them, and his sheep follow him because they know his voice. But they will never follow a stranger; in fact, they will run away from him because they do not recognize a stranger's voice" (John 10:4–5).

God is your shepherd, and He wants to guide you. He's going to lead you if you let Him. Hearing His voice isn't just something you can hope will happen; you can believe it *does*. Already. Right now. "They know his voice." It's part of following Him.

Did you get that? Our inability to hear doesn't mean it's not happening. It means something else is standing in the way.

3. God is always speaking to you.

God is constantly talking to His sheep, even when only a few are listening! This truth might represent a paradigm shift for you. You need to anchor it deep in your core. Set it like a post-in-cement, not-going-anywhere kind of belief.

God is a communicator. He is the original Word: "In the beginning was the Word, and the Word was with God, and the Word was God" (John 1:1). And He came to earth to communicate with us. "The Word became flesh and made his dwelling among us" (v. 14). Wow! We are that important to Him! Also, think about it: Who would author a book containing thousands and thousands of words if He didn't like to communicate?

God is a talker. He's an extrovert. He's a people person.

I cannot stress how important this core belief is. Why? Because if you think God is hiding from *you* or not speaking to *you*, you will miss His voice. Increase your confidence by tweaking one common word in your thoughts. Instead of wondering, Will *God speak to me?* start believing, *God is speaking to me*, right now.

GIVE THE REST OF THIS BOOK A TRY

Hearing God speak to you at the deepest level gives your life meaning. Knowing your Creator communicates with you confirms you are profoundly known and loved. Your existence is intentional. You aren't here by accident. You're on a divine mission.

The first thing I'm going to ask you to do is to try my approach, which I'll explain in the coming chapters. If you want to hear from God and have found it difficult, it's time to adopt some new habits. My friend Jenna once said to me, "Your current habits are perfectly designed to give you the exact results you're having. If you want a different result, you're going to need a different approach." I'd never thought of it like that before. If I want to change, I must be willing to change. If I don't change, I most likely will be in the exact same spot a year from now.

If I want to change, I must be willing to change.

Here's the deal: You don't have to conform to what others are doing or how they hear from God. But you must have the guts to show up as yourself. You must discover the way God works to get your attention, then get really good at recognizing it through practice. When you're clear about the way God approaches you, you'll know without a doubt when He's speaking to you.

I'm going to spend the rest of this book showing you how to do it. Trust me—it'll be crystal clear.

If you honor God's design for you, you'll be able to unlock all sorts of amazing things in your life. If it sounds too good to be true, I promise it's not! Step out of your comfort zone and take a risk. If you come to the end and feel let down, you can go back to what you've always done. But if you dare to test this method, you might wake up one day living the prophetic life you've always dreamed of. All you have to do is start right where you are.

Listen, I don't care if you think you're behind on your faith journey or that your faith life is completely broken. That you haven't given up trying to hear God matters! Don't get caught in the trap of *should'ves* or *could'ves*. Be here, in this book, with me now. Your faith life is a journey, not a destination.

What have you got to lose? Don't let your past mistakes, disappointments, or failures hold you back. Take a chance, push past your fears and doubts, and act. Stop wandering around on the outside looking in, feeling you will never be counted among those who hear from God. Come with me through the following chapters, and you'll never again underestimate the power of God in your life.

Because you were never created to do life alone, you need the voice of God in your everyday life. Here's the good news: You were made to communicate with your Creator, and it's within your design. Even better, God's speaking to you, and He's speaking your language.

Let's get started.

THE PROPHETIC
PERSONALITIES

DISCOVER THE HEARER

Then Eli realized that the LORD was calling the boy. So
Eli told Samuel, "Go and lie down, and if he calls you,
say, 'Speak, LORD, for your servant is listening.'"

—1 SAMUEL 3:8–9

I'VE MENTIONED MY TWIN SISTER, DEBORAH. I HAVEN'T
mentioned that we are identical twins. In fact, we are mirror twins.
Twenty-five percent of identical twins are mirror twins, which
means we mirror features. I'm a lefty, and she's a righty. Our hair
naturally parts on opposite sides. I'm cute, she's—

You know, stuff like that. We've lived similar stories for most of
our lives. Married six months apart, our first babies were born nine
days apart, our second babies are six weeks apart, and our third kids
were born three months apart. Crazy, right?

We live in different places but recently spent a week together. We
stayed in the same hotel, attended the same meetings, held conversations with the same people. Get this: we were surprised to find out

we were even reading the same book. While on the trip, we watched the same movie together, walked the same streets, and responded to the same invitation for prayer after hearing the same message.

But Deborah and I don't typically hear God speak to us in the same way. I have heard, seen, and felt God speaking to me, but the primary way that we communicate is through Knowing (more on this to come). Deborah hears God speak to her with words and phrases all the time.

She started one morning by telling me, "So last week while I was waking up, I heard the phrase *new season*. I felt like God was telling me He was taking me into a new season. Then last night, while we were at the service during worship, the worship leader began to sing about a new season. Immediately I heard the Lord say, *Deborah, I'm taking you into a new season. Get ready!* After the service, our host stopped me and said God had given her a word for me. She asked if she could share it with me. Of course, I agreed. She said, 'God is taking you into a new season. New spaces are coming your way. Get ready for expansion.' I was overwhelmed because that's exactly what I had been hearing God speak to me."

As Deb was sharing this, I was partly thinking, *Wow! Are you serious? That's more than I've heard all year!*

She continued, "After all of this, when we got in the car to leave, the song on the radio was about new seasons. God keeps confirming this word to me!"

I'm always in awe of how much God speaks verbally to Deborah. I went to the same church service, met the same lady, sang the same song, and sat in the same car, but I didn't get anything from God like that!

If you asked her, Deborah could give you a play-by-play each day of how God speaks to her all day long. He is always sharing something with her, as if He's telling her a story in real time. She has filled many, many journals with all the things God has spoken to her.

Deborah is a Hearer.

What It's Like Being a Hearer

- **HEARERS** receive the voice of God through words, phrases, and sentences.
- **HEARERS** seemingly have a direct line to God.
- God's distinct voice interrupts **HEARERS'** thoughts.
- **HEARERS** experience God's words in real time, in a play-by-play style.
- **HEARERS** know precisely what God said, when He said it, and where He said it.
- **HEARERS'** faith in what they know God said to them is strong.
- **HEARERS** learn from God through conversations with Him.
- **HEARERS** have a keen sense of confidence in what God is saying.
- Once **HEARERS** activate the word in their life, nothing can stop them.
- Once **HEARERS** hear God speak, they are immediately filled with courage.
- God relies on **HEARERS** to record His words.
- **HEARERS** love to keep a record of things through journaling and/or storytelling.

UNDERSTANDING THE HEARER

In the first part of this book, I used the term *hearing God* generally to refer to all the ways a believer might receive messages from the Lord. In these next two parts of the book, I use the word *hearing* to refer specifically to the Prophetic Personality of the Hearers.

Hearers are the most commonly recognized Prophetic Personality type. Most books, sermons, and podcasts about hearing God's voice are directed to the Hearers. Teachings about God speaking usually focus on His words, phrases, or conversations. Don't believe me? Google it. You'll see it right away.

If you're a Hearer, God shows up in your world through clear words and phrases. He might even speak to you in complete sentences. Hearers can pinpoint what God said, when He said it, and how it affected them. They often say things such as, "I heard God say . . ." or "God told me . . ." As a Hearer you encounter the voice of God through a play-by-play experience. At any given moment, you have a keen sense of what He is saying.

It's a powerful gift! We sit back in awe when a Hearer communicates what God is speaking, because the message is so clear.

Because Hearing is the most commonly taught of the Prophetic Personalities, most Hearers believe everyone experiences the voice of God in the same way. Doesn't everyone have conversations with Him? Nope, not at all. You might be surprised to learn this is just one way of getting messages from God.

But if you are a Hearer, He has given you a direct means of perceiving His voice and the words He wants you to help deliver to the world. Hearers beautifully encounter the voice of God as a direct dialogue with the heart of God, from the mouth of God. The more you listen and obey His voice, the more you have an anointing to share what He says with others. It's no wonder the church has elevated this Prophetic Personality.

Hearers beautifully encounter the voice of God as a direct dialogue with the heart of God, from the mouth of God.

As a Hearer, you hear God with an inner voice that interrupts your thoughts. At first you may think you aren't hearing God speak because what you hear doesn't sound super spiritual or relevant to you. But then something happens in your life that immediately takes you back to the moment you heard that word or phrase. It grounds you. You begin to recognize He's speaking to you, which builds your confidence in hearing Him.

For example, God will interrupt you in the middle of something you're doing. You think it's just your thoughts until you realize it has nothing to do with what you were thinking about. God's voice is always smarter and clearer than your thoughts!

Sometimes He will give you words and phrases for someone else. If you bravely share the words as God directs you, you can encourage others and give them clarity about what He is saying. It can literally change their lives.

But being a Hearer has its downsides. Because you hear God so clearly, others might develop unreasonably high expectations of you. They might hold you to an impossible standard. Some might become overdependent on you to tell them what God is saying rather than developing their own ability to receive messages from God and relying on Him. Because of your clear hearing, you might feel a heavy burden of being held accountable for every word you say, when you need space and grace to grow your gift just like everyone else does.

My friend Amy told me this story one morning as we walked together. God had spoken clearly to her husband, Keith, that they were to go plant a church together. Amy agreed. "We had a direct word from God," she said. They packed up their little family and moved across the country. Never admitting it at the time, they both expected it to be easy. After all, God had spoken to them directly.

Instead, they experienced the exact opposite. Nothing was easy. Life was incredibly difficult. Even with all their effort, planning, and sacrifice, nothing seemed to be working. Amy said, "After two years, our church's growth had come to a standstill. We had depleted our financial resources, drained our energy, and exhausted our strategic plans."

Living under so much stress took a toll on their marriage. Amy and Keith began to have more conflict. "I would blame Keith for moving me away from my family. Keith would blame me for not having faith in him. We were in a terrible place."

One night, after a huge argument, Amy called a trusted friend. She told me, "I picked this specific friend because I thought she'd agree with me." Her unashamed confession caught me by surprise. We both burst into laughter. You know how it is, right? Yeah, girl, we do!

"I unloaded on my friend, divulging everything. The word. The move. The defeat. Finally, taking a breath, I waited for her response. But it was not like anything I expected."

Her friend said, "Amy, you said God told Keith to plant this church, right?" Amy agreed. "When I asked you how you knew you should plant the church, you told me God had spoken to Keith. Am I still tracking?" Again Amy confirmed, not sure where this was going.

"Well, why did you move across the country to start a church without God speaking to *you* about it?" Amy was now listening to every word. "Friend, when did you lose your power? When did you stop hearing God for yourself and start hearing God only through Keith?"

Her friend's words pierced like a knife to the heart. She was right. Amy had surrendered her conviction, clarity, and decision-making to another human rather than looking to her divine source. She had elevated Keith's hearing to the point where she had stopped listening for herself.

Why is this experience important for a Hearer? The point is that Hearers can find themselves in Keith's shoes. Sometimes those around you, like Amy, become so dependent on your hearing they stop listening or contributing for themselves. They give away their power! This leaves you feeling alone in the process. In extreme situations you might feel more used for your "hearing" than respected for your personhood.

BIBLICAL HEARERS

God has never hesitated to use words, phrases, and dialogue to speak to His people. We see accounts of this in both the Old and New Testaments.

Before Jesus came to earth, God spoke through individuals as conduits of His voice. People such as Noah, Jacob, David, and Jonah heard the voice of God and shared it with people on earth. God gave them a special ability to hear His words and assignments to share them.

One of the clearest examples is in the first book of Samuel.

The boy Samuel ministered before the LORD under Eli. In those days the word of the LORD was rare; there were not many visions.

One night Eli, whose eyes were becoming so weak that he could barely see, was lying down in his usual place. The lamp of God had not yet gone out, and Samuel was lying down in the house of the LORD, where the ark of God was. Then the LORD called Samuel.

Samuel answered, "Here I am." And he ran to Eli and said, "Here I am; you called me."

But Eli said, "I did not call; go back and lie down." So he went and lay down.

Again the LORD called, "Samuel!" And Samuel got up and went to Eli and said, "Here I am; you called me."

"My son," Eli said, "I did not call; go back and lie down."

Now Samuel did not yet know the LORD: The word of the LORD had not yet been revealed to him.

A third time the LORD called, "Samuel!" And Samuel got up and went to Eli and said, "Here I am; you called me."

Then Eli realized that the LORD was calling the boy. So Eli told Samuel, "Go and lie down, and if he calls you, say, 'Speak, LORD, for your servant is listening.'" So Samuel went and lay down in his place.

The LORD came and stood there, calling as at the other times, "Samuel! Samuel!"

Then Samuel said, "Speak, for your servant is listening." (1 Sam. 3:1–10)

Samuel was a Hearer.

The New Testament offers other clear examples. The Pharisee Saul became the apostle Paul after the voice of Jesus asked him from heaven, "Why do you persecute me?" (Acts 9:4). Peter had a conversation with God about what food was acceptable for Jews to eat

(Acts 11:7–10). John heard the voice of God repeatedly as he received His revelation.

When Jesus promised the presence of God would come to His followers after He was gone, He signaled an important change to the status quo. God no longer wanted to speak only through certain individuals but to each of us. He does this by the gift of the Holy Spirit. "And I will ask the Father, and he will give you another advocate to help you and be with you forever—the Spirit of truth" (John 14:16–17). Another name for the Spirit of truth is the Holy Spirit. "When he, the Spirit of truth, comes, he will guide you into all the truth. He will not speak on his own; he will speak only what he hears, and he will tell you what is yet to come" (John 16:13).

The Bible promises the gift of the Holy Spirit to everyone who commits their life to Christ (Acts 2:38). Why is this important? Because among His divine roles, the Holy Spirit is the voice of God in your life, consistently allowing you to hear Him speak to you anytime and anywhere.

As a Hearer, if you act upon the words He's speaking to you, your life will change!

THE RHEMA WORD OF GOD

Among the most frequent questions I get about the Prophetic Personalities, and specifically the hearing of words, are these: What about the Bible? Doesn't it contain all the words of God? Shouldn't the Bible be all we need?

The answer is yes and no.

Yes, the Bible contains the words of God, but it's much, much more than that. Did you know that within the sacred confines of that book, you'll discover the very essence of God? That's right, my friend. The Bible holds the very presence and nature of God. The Bible is living and active—it's alive! "For the word of God is alive and active. Sharper than any double-edged sword, it penetrates even to dividing soul and spirit, joints and marrow; it judges the thoughts and attitudes of the heart" (Heb. 4:12).

As you dive deep into reading your Bible and consume the words of God, you'll embark on a journey of spiritual growth and experience a connection with the Divine that is unparalleled. The insights and teachings contained within the pages of your Bible have the power to transform your life. The Bible acts as our rock-solid foundation, providing profound wisdom and the answers to life.

Every believer has this incredible gift: full access to the divine wisdom of God through Scripture. It's like a treasure trove, the purest and safest path to uncovering the very thoughts and heart of the Almighty. But hold on tight, because here's where it gets even more mind-blowing: the Holy Spirit, the supernatural being within us, breathes truth and understanding not only through the sacred words of the Bible but also through the unique lens of our Prophetic Personalities.

This is important for Hearers. You have a special knack for hearing those *rhema* words of God—those quickened and specific messages straight from the Holy Spirit. Let me tell you, these words are like mighty weapons that slice through confusion, fear, and doubt. They have the power to transform lives in the blink of an eye. A single rhema word can shift your entire existence, propelling you toward greatness and unraveling the mysteries that once held you back.

When God spoke to me in the car that day when I was seventeen, inviting me to follow Him, that was a rhema word. Though I don't typically hear phrases and sentences from God, on that day I did.

Let me be clear: Not everything a Hearer hears has such dramatic results. But you'll never know when the rhema words you receive will change everything. Your only responsibility is to listen, respond, and share the words God gives you according to His instructions. So relax! Obedience is in your court; the outcome is in God's.

> **Obedience is in your court; the outcome is in God's.**

LEARNING BY LISTENING

Get this: the word *hearer* means "those who learn by listening." If you are a Hearer, then you're learning to hear the voice of God by listening to what He's saying and communicating those words to others. As you learn to hear God's voice, practice hearing Him speak through words, phrases, sentences, and conversations.

When God gives you a word, you'll probably want to revisit that word again and again.

It may be a word that helps you make an important decision, like where to live or what career path to follow. It may be a word that gives specific insight into someone else's life or situation. Or it could be a word that confirms God's timing, communication, and love for you.

You might see this word written somewhere (like in a social media post or magazine) or hear it spoken by someone who uses it in some way that feels significant for your life. You may find the word being repeatedly used around you. Whenever God gives you an important word, it will stand out from everything else going on around you, because it will have meaning for your life.

Hearing a word from God can stir up your emotions. You might feel a sense of peace or excitement, or you might feel an urgency to act. You might feel overwhelmed by the importance of what God has just shown you. These emotions are very important. Don't ignore them! As a Hearer, you will receive a word that evokes a feeling. (This is different from Feelers, who receive messages through emotions rather than words; more on them a bit later.) Experiencing a "feeling after hearing" can help confirm and guide you in determining whether you are truly hearing God's word for your life.

Here's an interesting fact: you are likely to have a more difficult time hearing God's word for your own life than for others. What?! It's true, because as much as you want to believe you have the purest intentions, it's almost impossible for you to think of your own life objectively. That doesn't make you bad; it makes you human.

So, to protect and confirm the word in your life, it's important to learn how to test the words you get. This is true for everyone but especially Hearers. I've outlined how to do this in chapter 14.

JOURNALING FOR YOURSELF AND OTHERS

It's common for Hearers to be devoted journal keepers.

You love to write down what God is speaking to you. You have a natural inclination to recognize and preserve these divine messages through writing. No matter what challenges come your way, you are committed to documenting these moments of your life. Even when doubts try to cast shadows on your experiences, you hold on to the deep knowing that these divine interactions are genuine and significant.

Your trusted companion, the journal, is an essential tool for affirming your spiritual journey. Through the simple act of writing, you find peace, validation, and a profound sense of purpose. Each entry in your journal serves as a testament to your personal growth and as a tangible reminder that God's voice has been guiding your path all along.

You may have stacks of journals documenting years of your life. What a wonderful record of your history with Him! Writing things down isn't just a hobby, though. It's super important if you're a Hearer. Throughout history Hearers faithfully wrote down what they heard, believing that it would be important later. Think about it: if Isaiah, Jeremiah, Paul, John, and others hadn't written down what God said to them, we wouldn't have the complete content of the Word of God that we have today.

Imagine how your life will change when you find out what the voice of God is saying to you. Picture your life transforming before your very eyes as you tap into the extraordinary power of hearing God's voice. Just imagine: You're engrossed in a book when suddenly, the Divine interrupts your thoughts, revealing your next step. Or perhaps you're deep in prayer, seeking answers, and then *boom!* The voice of God breaks through, providing the solution to your most pressing problem. Even in the midst of parenting chaos, unsure of how to navigate, the voice of God effortlessly interrupts, presenting you with the long-awaited strategy you've been desperate for.

Prepare to embark on a journey where divine interruptions become the catalyst for your miraculous transformation.

DISCOVER THE SEER

Before David got up the next morning, the word of
the LORD had come to Gad the prophet, David's seer.

−2 SAMUEL 24:11

BRITNEY CAME FROM A BROKEN FAMILY.

Her mom, a single working woman, worked three jobs to
make ends meet. Britney and her brothers never met their father,
but everything they heard confirmed they weren't missing much.
Britney was a survivor. She'd single-handedly dug herself out of the
systemic poverty, abuse, and environment that made her vulnerable
to getting stuck.

Britney was the first one in her family to graduate college. She'd
learned how to persevere. Dig deep. Make stuff happen. But even
after all the effort and success, she sensed deep down she was missing something.

A friend from work invited Britney to a church service one
evening. She had no idea how it would radically change her life.

That night she found God . . . or He found her. Just as she did with everything else in her life, Britney threw herself into her relationship with Jesus. She began reading her Bible, learning to pray, and surrounding herself with a community of believing friends who helped to nurture and support her newfound belief.

One night while driving home from work, Britney noticed a building on a street corner available for lease. Never having noticed this building before, she was surprised it stood out. When she looked at it, she immediately saw a picture of it in her mind's eye. It was renovated, featuring a little café and a place to create a boutique too. It seemed so real to her, as if she could almost touch it—as if the renovation had already happened. The image wasn't some vague, grainy, black-and-white idea. It was vivid and detailed, full of color and emotion. She could see the walls, the floor. She could smell the food, hear the laughter in the air, feel the warmth of lit candles on the tables.

At home, she brushed off the image as little more than a great idea. But as the days went on, she couldn't shake the feeling that the building was meant for her.

A year later, Britney learned that a coworker's uncle owned that building. Not knowing anything about Britney's vision, her colleague explained that his uncle was looking for someone willing to turn it into a business for the community.

Britney's creative wheels started turning, though she lacked confidence. *Am I crazy? Who am I to want to start a business?* Britney was conflicted. She had no plan B. She didn't have a trust fund to pick up the pieces if she failed. But something arose in her: faith! She thought, *I'll just start knocking on doors and see what opens.*

Door after door swung wide open.

Almost two years later, she held the keys to her business venture. She was as enthusiastic as she was terrified. Mostly, she was excited.

Not everyone was as excited as Britney. Her friends expressed real concerns. When her idea for the business was just an idea, no one questioned her, but as Britney quit her job, acquired a business loan, and began to invest all her time and resources in the new business, they started speaking up.

"Britney, we're happy for you, but we're also really concerned. I mean, how are you going to get people to visit your restaurant? You're a smart girl, but you don't have any experience in the food industry. We love you. We believe in you, but we just can't see how it's going to happen."

Her mom's voice joined theirs: "Honey, what are you doing opening a café? Do you really know what you're doing? You've worked so hard to get your degree. Why throw it all away for a picture in your head?"

Britney tried not to let their concerns bother her, but they still stung. After all, she hadn't been searching for a vision that day she drove by the building for lease. She hadn't created the image in her head and then mustered the faith to believe it. No, she had received her vision divinely, and it had been accompanied by faith. She felt as if the vision was pulling her forward into the future.

The funny thing was, if you were to ask Britney about short-term plans, such as what she was having for dinner that night, she probably wouldn't be able to tell you. But if you asked her about long-term dreams such as her restaurant, she had every detail meticulously planned.

A little more than three years after she drove by the empty building, Britney pulled into the parking lot to prepare for her grand opening. Everything she had seen in her mind was now a reality. Her vision—accompanied by faith, a few years, teary-eyed moments, and terrifying risks—had finally come to pass.

Britney is a Seer.

What It's Like Being a Seer

- God speaks to **SEERS** in dreams, daydreams, pictures, images, and visions.
- **SEERS** see the world differently.
- **SEERS** perceive what God is doing and will do, but not necessarily how.
- **SEERS** see things as complete or finished from the very beginning.
- When **SEERS** see something, they envision what is supposed to happen.
- **SEERS'** dreams and visions can be too big to accomplish without God.
- **SEERS** are filled with great faith that what they see will come to pass.
- **SEERS** get a vision that encompasses their passion and motivates them.
- **SEERS** know there are no boundaries around what God can do.
- **SEERS** can see beyond what most people can see.
- **SEERS** have supernatural ideas and solutions.
- **SEERS** see what heaven sees and have an aerial view of God's purpose.

UNDERSTANDING THE SEER

God shows up in the Seer's world visually through mental images, dreams, visions, and even daydreams. These visions don't always seem supernatural or especially spiritual. Sometimes they are about mundane, day-to-day issues.

If you're a Seer, God shows you these things to reveal His nearness and investment in your life. You see the world differently; that is, you see things as they could be, not only as they are. You have an eye for the future. You love to dream big. You can inspire others to see what is possible and stir them to action.

When Seers encounter a picture from God, they become visionaries—dreamers filled with faith. You're more than a strategic leader who draws people toward what might happen. You also see through the lens of faith: "It's *going to happen.*" Seers have a powerful ability to see things at long distances, which gives you a unique perspective. You see with spiritual eyes what God is doing or will do.

When Seers encounter a picture from God, they become visionaries–dreamers filled with faith.

But as a Seer you face a significant battle.

Others might not find your perspective easy to understand. Sometimes it's difficult to explain what you see or why it matters. It's hard to get people on board with the big ideas. Most Seers go through seasons of life when they feel like no one is listening to them.

Maybe you already know what this is like. You've tried to express your passion to somebody, but they just can't grasp what you're talking about. You may have felt frustrated that they didn't understand or care about what's most important to you. It's a deflating experience.

Seers envision destinies and dream big dreams. They love to strategize with the Lord to bring their visions to pass. They are captivated by the possibilities of what could be. You may even have prophetic dreams and visions (that is, foreknowledge of specific events).

My friend Tony is a Seer. "I'm the big-picture guy," he often says. "I'm the pack-up-your-family-and-move-overseas-just-because-I saw-it guy. The best way to describe how God speaks to me is like this: He puts a pair of glasses on me, and I see everything in my life through those special lenses. Through them I can receive information, prophetic words, and scriptures. I can get advice for strangers and friends. But ultimately, my inner voice says, *I see through these lenses, and I know exactly where I'm going, and I'm not changing direction.*"

When Seers catch sight of what God is trying to show them, they're instantly filled with a sense of wonder and anticipation for the possibilities. They think, *Now I see it! This is where I'm going and what I'm doing. This is what I'm building. This is what I'm destined to do. This is my purpose.*

Seers might spot these visions anywhere, at any time. God might give you a spiritual picture during corporate worship or a prayer time, but His communication isn't limited to a church setting.

The Seer is also known for having unique pictures and perspectives about people and situations. You are often good at making connections between different ideas or concepts that other people might not see. The Seer is especially adept at seeing patterns in life, relationships, and nature; you may see what others miss entirely.

Jennifer explained it like this: "Last week a friend of mine reached out because she had a problem. She needed to find a solution in prayer. I prayed for her, and as I prayed, I saw a picture of her as a little girl playing on a swing with her dad. I heard the Lord saying that her dad is her safe place. I shared what I saw and said, 'I think you should go to your father. I believe he will have the solution for your situation.' She was surprised because her dad *is* her safe place, and she had already set up a meeting with him to discuss the problem."

BIBLICAL SEERS

The Bible records so many instances of God speaking to His people through dreams and visions that I couldn't possibly list them all in this space. I'd need a whole other book. We don't know why He liked this method so much, but it must be a good one because He used it all the time. Obviously, God uses whatever means is the most effective way of getting His message across. Theologian John Loren Sandford believed that dreams and visions occupy more than one-third of the Old Testament.[1] The book of Job says, "He speaks in dreams, in visions of the night, when deep sleep falls on people as they lie in their beds" (33:15 NLT). Still, God's communication with the early church is almost exclusively through dreams and visions (see the book of Acts).

Keeping all that in mind, I'll offer up a few biblical examples.

- Samuel and Gad were Seers, which meant they could see with spiritual eyes what God was doing and what He would do. They had a spiritual gift for perceiving the meaning of things that were unknown to everyone else (1 Chron. 29:29).

- Jacob dreamed of a ladder stretching up into heaven (Gen. 28:12).
- Joseph, the son of Jacob, dreamed of his future (Gen. 37:1–10).
- Solomon asked for wisdom in a dream (1 Kings 3:5–9).
- Three times God appeared to Joseph, the earthly father of Jesus, in dreams (Matt. 1:20; 2:13, 19–20).
- People who had visions of heaven include Paul (2 Cor. 12:2), Stephen (Acts 7:55–56), and John (Rev. 1:12–16).
- God used visions to tell Paul where to go (Acts 16:9).

If God communicated in dreams throughout Scripture, why would He stop now? He hasn't. God is the same today as He was yesterday (Heb. 13:8).

VISUAL MOMENTS

A couple of years ago I was preaching when I suddenly saw a mental picture of a piece of paper. On it was written the word *report*, and the word was being crossed out.

God impressed upon me the need to stress *three days*. I felt the Holy Spirit in it. I said to those in the room and those watching online, "I feel like the Lord wants you to know that the reports are being canceled in the next three days." Then I saw a hand with rings on it. I said, "I see people are getting engaged in the next three days. People are getting jobs in the next three days. Things are coming to fruition in the next three days."

I finished with, "Please email us if anything happens to you within three days."

Emails flooded my inbox. Messages flooded my social accounts.

"I got the job." "I got the apartment." "I got the man." People sent pictures of rings on their left hand. Everyone was so happy!

In the past I wouldn't have been sure the picture was from God. It didn't take over my eyesight. I wasn't overcome by supernatural emotion. A couple of pictures quickly entered my mind's eye. I could have dismissed them, but I knew they were from God.

How did I know? I had learned through practice and risk-taking.

Remember my experience at age seventeen at the conference in Southern California, where I first tapped into my sense of God speaking to me? I took a risk, and God confirmed He was the source of what I had perceived.

After that I practiced being on the alert for God's messages to me. I practiced *a lot.* I started by sharing what I received with close friends and family. Sometimes I got a picture, a word, or even a phrase. Sometimes I would experience a deep desire to pray for someone. I would have a dream about a person that felt significant. Though I felt nervous to share it with them, I'd do it anyway. Sometimes they would thank me but say it didn't mean anything. Other times what I shared elicited a powerful response. It impacted them deeply. They would confirm I had heard from God, because only He knew certain details I had disclosed and their significance.

Practicing and taking risks was the only way to confirm I was perceiving God accurately. I did this at every opportunity, day after day, year after year, until I established a rich history with God. Now when He speaks to me in any mode, I can immediately recognize that it's Him. I know His "voice" even when it is an image.

The night I saw that picture, I knew it was a divine picture from God. When I saw it I was filled with faith to declare it. It was just crazy, and God covered me. Thank You, God!

BIG VISIONS

Stop right where you are and look around.

Are you sitting in a building?

Are you outside at the park?

Maybe you're driving somewhere, listening to this book in an audio format.

No matter where you are, if you look hard enough, you will spot evidence of a Seer.

Someone saw what you see *before* it was created. Someone who dreamed big! Creating that thing may have taken them a lifetime. Maybe they didn't even get to see the completion of the project. But you get to experience the results of a big vision.

Seers see what's not there—*yet*! Seers are missional. You are the Marco Polo of the spirit world. Once Seers see a vision, everything they do from that point is in support of the vision.

"We're going to feed this many people."

"We're going to get them water over here."

"We're going to build this building (or house or orphanage)."

When you show others the picture God has given you, they are filled with faith too. It's contagious!

If you are a Seer, you will often experience faith-filling moments as you view what God is saying to you. His message might seem impossible to your natural eyes, but when you see with your spiritual eyes, you are filled with faith and hope for the impossible.

When you show others the picture God has given you, they are filled with faith too. It's contagious! You can inspire others to move forward boldly, to believe they can reach new heights and embark on new journeys. You unite others to take one giant leap forward and believe for the impossible together.

Mature Seers ensure the visions become a reality. You're good at constructing clear goals, describing a strategic plan to achieve them, and empowering others to act on them. When you accept God's vision, there are no limitations on what He can do through you. I love this part about Seers. The world needs you!

NIGHT DREAMS

A man I knew had a dream of being given a million dollars by someone he barely knew. He kept that dream in his heart and told only a few people about it. Sixteen years later, when he needed to pay off a church building debt, he received a million dollars from the person he saw in the dream. That dream had never died in his heart.

Why does God speak to us in our dreams? The answer may be in the findings of neuroscience. (Let me remind you, God and science are not separate. Real science always reveals the evidence of a real God.)

What is neuroscience? It's the study of the brain and its impact on behavior and cognitive functions, or how people think. Neuroscience tells us that visual imagery is one of the most efficient human communication tools.[2] Humans can identify and understand pictures with breathtaking speed—far faster than we can process written or spoken words.[3] (Maybe that explains why we're constantly being targeted by advertisers and marketers with pictures. You think?)

Pastor Tania Harris wrote:

Dreams and visions usually place visuals into the context of a story. This has an even greater impact on our brains. MRI scans tell us that when we watch a story unfold, we process it as participants rather than spectators. Not only does the dream engage the language part of our brains, but it also activates the parts we would normally use if we were actually experiencing it. What's more, when we see images in our mind, the chemicals associated with emotions are released into our bodies. This has an impact on our physiology and neural pathways. It effectively changes us. The impact is felt throughout our bodies, emotions, and minds.[4]

Have you ever woken up from a dream that felt so real it took you a minute to gather yourself? Maybe you dream someone is trying to kill you. When you wake up, your heart is pounding, you're sweaty, and you feel panicked. You feel an extreme sense of relief as you discover it was only a dream.

Worse yet, you have a dream that your significant other is cheating on you. You wake up feeling betrayed and angry. (Anyone? Asking for a friend.) It might feel confusing to have all these emotions when it was just a dream. The dream seems so real that it engages all your senses. It affects you psychologically and physically!

The Bible confirms dreams can be strong communication channels from heaven. As we sleep, God opens our inner eyes and provides us with insight and instructions. He's telling us what to do. But not every dream is from God; some are the result of the slice of pizza you had before you went to sleep. So you must weigh each dream and be discerning. Why would God communicate with you when you're sleeping? Maybe because you're not distracted by your daily duties. God can give you a clear message from beginning to end.

My friend David explains, "When I was figuring out what to study, I had a dream in the night where I saw an earthquake happening. There was so much confusion. Parents were looking for their kids, who were hidden. When I woke up, I felt a longing to work with kids so they would have an encounter and would be saved. Often, I get pictures when I ask the Lord for a prophetic word. I have a clear picture in my inner eyes of a vision for my life."

God often shows Seers His messages in dreams. He gives an answer to a question, a solution to a problem, or a word of hope for a hopeless situation.

MUSTARD-SEED VISIONS

When Seers receive a picture from God, it has the potential to grow from its initial mustard-seed state into something the whole world can experience.

Take your ability to see seriously. Imagine all the people you will touch. How many lives could be changed because you gave them insight into what God sees? Likewise, imagine how many things will never happen if you don't acknowledge the images God is giving you. Consider that the pictures you're receiving aren't just thoughts or ideas but God's very rhema word. He's directly speaking to you. He's trying to communicate with you! Don't ignore Him. You'll miss what He wants for you and the world. And so will everyone else.

Your seeing carries a legacy for your children and your children's children. You possess a piece of the puzzle that God is assembling. He needs someone to see the future with Him, to dream the dreams He dreams, and that's you!

DISCOVER THE FEELER

You have turned my mourning into joyful dancing.

–PSALM 30:11 NLT

A FEW MONTHS BEFORE I TURNED TWENTY-ONE, I GOT an unexpected phone call.

"Havilah, I have a question for you."

It took a minute for my brain to register who was calling. Oh— Mr. Perry! He was a family friend and a relative by marriage, a successful businessman who attended a church I regularly visited.

"I want you and your sister to come to Israel with my family as our guests," he announced.

Surprised and delighted, Deborah and I agreed to go. We sensed God was giving us this trip as a birthday gift. Three months later we were landing in Tel Aviv and joining a group of forty others for a two-week tour. My sister and I were the youngest on the trip by at least a decade. But it didn't matter to us because we were having a fantastic time!

Deb and I weren't the Perrys' only guests. Two other women came as well. I'll call them Julie and Claire. We four became fast friends. Julie and Claire were leaders in their churches, overseeing the prophetic and intercessory gifts, and they added a rich spiritual element to our tour. Each day our bus arrived at a site where we would walk around together, listening to the tour guide and spending time praying and reflecting. I quickly became aware that these two women were having experiences completely different from mine.

Both women were visibly affected by these sites. With deep emotions—sometimes laughter, sometimes tears, sometimes amazement—they explained what God was speaking to them. They told us what they were feeling and what they felt we should pray for. Clearly, they were having a very moving experience.

None of this bothered me until they started to direct their attention to me. They often said things like, "Can you feel what God is doing right now? Wow! It's really intense," or "Can't you just feel God in this place? It's incredible!" At first, I casually agreed. After all, I was in Israel! Nobody wants to look like a heathen in Israel. But as they shared their insights day after day with fervency, emotions, and tears, I tried to deflect their attention.

Finally, a week into the tour, I couldn't take it anymore. When they asked me what I was sensing, I blurted, "I feel nothing. In fact, I haven't felt anything this whole time. The only thing I've really felt is that I want a falafel." My answer startled them. I looked them in the eyes, bracing for judgment, but instead they burst into laughter!

The women weren't laughing at me, though. They quickly explained that they had never expected me to feel what they were feeling. They apologized for unintentionally pressuring me into their experience. I took a deep breath and felt relieved. Clearly God was speaking to them in profound ways and with deep emotions, but that had nothing to do with me.

Julie and Claire were Feelers.

What It's Like Being a Feeler

- God speaks to **FEELERS** through emotions and sensations.
- **FEELERS** have unusual sensitivity to their surroundings.
- **FEELERS** sense what God is saying by experiencing His emotions.
- **FEELERS'** emotions give insight into what's going on in the heart of God.
- **FEELERS** perceive spiritual nuances that most people miss.
- **FEELERS** can't explain why they feel something. They just do.
- God interrupts **FEELERS** through their emotions so they can partner with Him.
- Mature **FEELERS** can feel something without being overcome by it.
- **FEELERS** will carry what they feel with them.
- **FEELERS** are powerful intercessors.
- **FEELERS'** emotions connect to the mystery of God's heart, motives, and emotions.

UNDERSTANDING THE FEELER

If you are a Feeler, God speaks into your world through the spiritual conduit of intense emotions. Because we all feel emotion, many Feelers don't immediately recognize an emotional experience as God's communication. Some have even been taught that their feelings are untrustworthy or dangerous.

As a Feeler you reflect God's heart. You feel God's emotions in unusual ways. You are very sensitive to the tangible presence of God. Most of the time you feel things others don't feel. You often know where others are emotionally and spiritually, even when you don't seek out this information. This is because you have a unique openness to the emotions of God.

As a Feeler you live with a unique awareness of your surroundings. You can walk into an environment and sense any subtext in what's going on. You have likely been able to detect positively or negatively charged atmospheres since you were a child. You may remember a home, a school, a store, or even a church that didn't feel quite right.

You notice things others don't notice because your emotional connection to God runs below the surface of obvious things. This heightened sensitivity allows you to feel things that others cannot detect with their physical senses.

The heart is the seat of the emotions, and it's where Feelers sense God's presence. God has a heart, and so do you. God wants you to experience His heart in an unparalleled way.

A common misconception is that most Feelers are female. Let me stop you right there! Feelers are not emotional in the way expressive women are sometimes maligned. In fact, Feelers may not even always express their emotional connection to God in the way that, say, Julie and Claire did. A Feeler simply experiences the voice of God through a heart connection. You can sense the heart of God even when it runs contrary to your own personal feelings.

Feelers catch nuances most people miss. They can't always explain why they feel something, but they know what they feel.

My dad and husband are both Feelers. It's not uncommon to enter an environment with either of them and hear them say, "I just don't think we should be here," or "I feel like we need to pray." My dad says, "Whenever I hear a siren from an ambulance or fire engine, I get emotional and begin to pray. I think, *Someone's in trouble, I need to pray!*"

Late one night my dad was walking through the lobby of a hotel after ministering at a church. As he passed the night clerk, Dad sensed compassion and heard the Lord say, *Tell the night clerk that Jesus loves him.* Dad wanted to brush it off. He was tired and thought, *Oh, that is too simple. Everyone knows that.* But as he got to the elevator, the intensity of the compassion grew. He turned around and went back to give the clerk the message. When he did, the man broke down and began to weep. He said, "I've been asking for a sign from God all day!" That man's life was changed all because my dad responded to God pulling on his heartstrings.

Feelers have a keen sense of what's happening in the spirit world. Sometimes the feeling is positive and sometimes it's negative. It's clear you're feeling something outside your own emotions. God is speaking to you!

Feelers are used to being interrupted by God via their emotions. You'll be going through your day and suddenly be overwhelmed by a feeling. It could be sadness, heaviness, or a sense of incredible peace or joy. Sometimes it's a feeling that you need to do something specifically. The emotion compels you to listen and even to act.

Your feelings and emotions aren't broken. They are powerful

indicators of what God is speaking to and through you. God has made you this way.

WHAT GOD THINKS ABOUT FEELINGS

"Jesus wept" (John 11:35).

Have you ever considered why God would put this verse in the Bible? Jesus, who was fully God and fully man, had emotions just as you and I do. He allowed Himself to feel deeply, to cry, to feel anger, to feel compassion, and He allowed it all to be documented. He acknowledged and accepted His feelings. He wanted all who read the Bible to know emotions are important. I hope this releases you to acknowledge and experience your emotions too.

God can feel grief (Eph. 4:30). Joy is a fruit of the Spirit (Gal. 5:22). The justice of God can spark terror (Prov. 21:15). The Bible's wisdom literature extols the value of happiness (Eccl. 3:12). Godly sorrow can lead to repentance (2 Cor. 7:10). Hope in God can lead to calmness and contentment (Ps. 131).

Throughout church history God has not shied away from using Feelers.

George Whitefield was a catalyst for the First Great Awakening of the 1700s. He spoke to as many as ten million people. During some of his meetings, people would cry out and fall to the ground under the supernatural conviction of God. Author John Dunn describes Whitefield's passion:

> It was said of George Whitefield, that it was not uncommon for
> him to weep profusely in the pulpit when preaching, and some said
> that they hardly knew him to get through a sermon without some

tears. The great preacher felt so intensely for those to whom he was preaching that it often found an outlet in this way in tears—so much so, that his hearers found it hard to hate the man who wept so much over their souls. In one sermon he cried out: "If you will not weep over your own sins, then I will"! One man said of him: "I came to hear you with my pocket full of stones to break your head, but your sermon got the better of me and broke my heart."[1]

It wasn't until I dove deep into Scripture and heard from hundreds of people that I finally believed my findings were unmistakable: Feelers' experience of God is deeply connected to their emotions. God isn't neutral about our feelings, nor is He afraid of them. God doesn't speak only through words and images but also through our emotions. By allowing God to speak to us through our emotions, we experience God through the most fundamental expression of our hearts.

God isn't neutral about our feelings, nor is He afraid of them.

This might be a challenging claim, but stay with me. Let me unpack what I mean so we can stay healthy, safe, and biblical.

First, your emotions have no moral value.

This truth was an earthshaking revelation for me. Let's look at this verse together: "In your anger do not sin" (Eph. 4:26). Most of us misunderstand this passage because we think it means that anger is sin, but that's not what it says. It identifies anger and sin as *two different things*. This is important because if you believe that squashing your emotions is an indicator of your spiritual or moral health, you've had it wrong. (This is an easy mistake to make if you're not a very emotional person in the first place. Insert raising hand!) Paul was warning us not to *act* on the feeling of anger that can lead us to sin. He was not saying that anger itself is a sin.

Jesus got angry enough at the money changers in the temple to drive them out with a whip, overturn their tables, and scatter their coins (John 2:14–16). And we know Jesus was without sin (1 John 3:5). I think we've largely missed this as a faith culture. Your emotions have no moral value, but what you choose to do with those emotions does. All actions have consequences, for better or worse.

Second, your emotions are signals.

Like lights on a dashboard, your emotions give you insight into what's happening inside you. God gave you emotions to help you live a full life. They signal what needs your attention, such as negative thoughts or false beliefs. Your emotions are also powerful because they give you the ability to have empathy for others. They are the moving force that helps you love others well.

Regardless of what you've been taught or believed, your feelings are entirely yours. No one is powerful enough to go inside you and choose your feelings. God has given you ownership of your feelings. You have the right to feel whatever you want to feel, but once you feel it, what you choose to do with it is critical.

I love this popular saying often attributed to Jonatan Mårtensson: "Feelings are like waves. You can't keep them from coming, but you can decide which one to surf."

BIBLICAL FEELERS

In Scripture the word *heart* often includes all emotions, referring to that part of us that becomes stirred up when we are in love or angry or afraid or feeling joyful or sad. Jeremiah is widely known among biblical scholars as "the weeping prophet," though that term doesn't appear in the Bible. Jeremiah was often stirred up and moved to grief over the plight of Israel.

When Jesus' mother, Mary, visited her cousin Elizabeth, the two pregnant women were filled with joy and awe. The Bible says the Holy Spirit filled Elizabeth (Luke 1:41)! Elizabeth's baby (John the Baptist) leaped in her womb, and Mary praised God with a song that has become a source of joy for others ever since (Luke 1:46–55).

During His time on earth, Jesus often felt compassion for the crowds who had come to hear Him teach (Matt. 9:36). And when Jesus' time here was finished, He left behind 120 church members and 11 leaders (Acts 1:15). He had promised them that He was going to send a helper (John 14:16–17), and we now know that gift was the Holy Spirit.

When the Holy Spirit came to earth, His arrival shocked everybody. A huge wind filled the room. The Spirit looked like tongues of fire on each person's head, and everybody was filled with the Holy Spirit. This is what's happening when we read Acts 2:43: "And a sense of awe (reverential fear) came upon every soul, and many wonders and signs were performed through the apostles (the special messengers)" (AMPC).

When the Holy Spirit came in, everyone felt strong emotion. They shared a holy fear. They all experienced and encountered Him in such a way that it changed them. I love this!

HEART MOMENTS

As a Feeler, you experience God in a deeply personal way that tends to move your heart and emotions. In the beginning you feel a strong emotion and think, *Am I unstable? Is something wrong with me? Is this just a season in my life?* A woman might wonder, *Is it that time of the month?*

One of the first times I spoke publicly about Prophetic Personalities, a young man from the back of the room made a bee-line for me at the end of my message. He almost knocked me over with his enthusiasm, and he struggled to get his words out. But he finally said: "Miss Havilah, you just cleared up years of therapy. I thought something was wrong with me. But as you began to talk about the Feeler, I realized that's me! I'm not crazy. I just never understood why I felt so many things at different times. This has changed my life. Now I know I'm not unstable; I'm a Feeler."

Watching a Feeler finally have the validation that he is hearing God according to the way God designed him is powerful! God will interrupt you through your emotions to get your attention, but also to give you secrets from heaven. He wants to partner with you!

A former personal assistant of mine, Tiffany, was a Feeler. Many times as I prepared to speak I would ask what she was feeling in the room. Because she was a woman who walked with God, I always trusted her response. Without fail she would share something that I never would've noticed and did not feel myself. Tiffany was a great asset. God spoke to her in a way I don't usually experience, and her insight helped me view situations in new ways. I now seek out Feelers!

FEELERS AS INTERCESSORS

God wants each of us to be intercessors, but Feelers have a unique call to pray on behalf of others.

The word *intercede* comes from the Latin words *inter,* meaning "between," and *cedere,* meaning "to move" or "to go." So the most literal meaning of *intercede* is "go between."[2] In the context of prayer, to intercede is to go between God and someone else on their behalf. At the risk of oversimplifying the topic: we ask Him to intervene and to do what only He can do.[3]

Feelers have a unique call to pray on behalf of others.

Oswald Chambers, one of my favorite authors, wrote this about intercessory prayer: "Worship and intercession must go together; one is impossible without the other. Intercession means raising ourselves up to the point of getting the mind of Christ regarding the person for whom we are praying."[4]

What does this have to do with Feelers?

Because God speaks to you through deep emotions, it can be easy for you to feel burdened by what you sense. Feelings like empathy, compassion, and sympathy can accumulate and weigh you down. You're in danger of owning everything! It will sometimes seem like your emotions are piling on and overwhelming you. If you're not sure how to separate which emotions belong to God, you, or someone else, you'll be at risk of becoming confused and overwhelmed, even with the best intentions. I'll offer some guidance in chapter 11 on how to determine that.

You need a strategy to release emotions that aren't from God: intercession. When you feel strong emotions about someone or something, it may move you to be so overwhelmed with compassion that you feel helpless or powerless. But you are neither. Through intercession we step into the supernatural gap and experience God's power.

Jesus said His yoke is easy and His burden is light (Matt. 11:30).

We don't have to be weighed down by any of this. But if we are, He also said we can cast our worry and anxiety on Him, because He cares for us (1 Peter 5:7). Charles Spurgeon suggested that in Greek, the word *cast* represents the image of throwing something away from you with both hands. Pastor David Guzik calls these "the hand of prayer and the hand of faith" and quotes Charles Spurgeon as saying, "Prayer tells God what the care is, and asks God to help, while faith believes that God can and will do it. Prayer spreads the letter of trouble and grief before the Lord, and opens all its budget, and then faith cries, 'I believe that God cares, and cares for me; I believe that he will bring me out of my distress, and make it promote his own glory.'"[5]

In prayer we take all our burdens and feelings and everything God is giving us, and we throw them at the feet of Jesus! Beni Johnson, a pastor at Bethel Church until she passed in 2022, opened my eyes to this. She wrote in her book *The Happy Intercessor* about praying until we find joy again.

As a healthy Feeler, you will experience emotions and ask God if they are from Him. You can disown anything that's not from Him and give back any burden you've been carrying through prayer. It's a beautiful exchange!

If you never learn how to let God lead you as a Feeler, you might feel like you're broken. Your emotions may compel you to act out of pain, anxiety, or even fear. Life can feel very heavy if you don't know how to give back to God everything you feel. Overwhelming! Too much to bear! On the other hand, imagine what life would be like if you could not dismiss your emotions but identify and celebrate them, believing you're not broken, overly emotional, or just too much for God.

Imagine the freedom of experiencing emotions but not owning

everything you experience. Imagine feeling something for yourself or someone else and immediately knowing it's God's way of getting your attention. Imagine the depth of prayer you will experience as you connect with God's emotions. How many people will learn through you that God's not a robot? He's not a disconnected divine being but a real-time, hands-on God who experiences all emotions and whose heart bleeds for humanity. You have a profound gift!

SEVEN

DISCOVER THE KNOWER

"Who gives intuition to the heart
and instinct to the mind?"

—JOB 38:36 NLT

MEGAN SAT ON HER FRONT PORCH, WATCHING FOR signs of her husband Pete's car. She'd been on the phone with her sister Lena earlier in the day. They'd talked about the real estate market, which Lena was invested in, and the urgency to buy before prices increased. Lena's urgency had lit a fire under Megan; she had it all worked out. A house down the street had just hit the market. Luckily for Megan, she'd had her eye on it for some time.

After Pete got home and walked through the door, Megan, who had promised herself not to come on too strong, couldn't wait any longer. She passionately unfolded her plan. Pete listened. At the end of her monologue, Pete agreed to think about it. After all, Megan was great at making decisions, and Pete enjoyed that about her. Pete asked for time, and Megan agreed.

Pete didn't know Megan had already made up her mind. She'd run down the road in her thoughts, making plans for their big move. She was confident this was the right thing to do.

But everything came to a sudden halt when Pete said he didn't think they should buy just then. Megan was shocked, disappointed, and in disbelief. Why didn't Pete want to buy the house? Didn't he understand the critical state of the market? Hadn't she presented her case well enough?

Megan was confused. Pete had always said he wanted to buy a house, but now that they had the chance, he was saying no? "Don't you want a house?" she asked him.

He nodded. "I do. I totally get why you think it's time, and I'd love a house, really. But something inside me knows it isn't the right time."

Megan felt herself getting worked up. "Did God tell you we shouldn't buy the house? Did He speak to you? Because if He did, then—"

"No, I can't say God spoke to me," Pete admitted. "I didn't hear Him say anything. I just have a sense that it isn't the right time."

Megan was disappointed, but she knew if she pushed, Pete would give in to her demands. She recalled learning in their pre-marriage class that "You need two yeses in a marriage to make one solid yes." So she begrudgingly shelved the conversation.

No more than a year after that, in 2008, the US housing market crashed. Houses dropped in value, and people owed more than the houses were worth. Half of Pete and Megan's friends had to take steep losses on their homes, and some even filed for bankruptcy. It was devastating. But Megan and Pete had escaped the devastation. Megan quickly connected the dots: Pete had sensed the voice of God. He was right—they were not supposed to purchase a home at that time.

Pete had heard from God, but not audibly. And he didn't use the words "God told me."

In their early years of marriage, Megan would have been the first to say she was the more spiritual one. She often sensed what God was saying, felt His tangible presence, and was quick to tell others. Deep down, Megan assumed Pete didn't have as deep a faith as she did.

But now, after almost twenty years of marriage, Megan understands she was dead wrong. Pete had been listening to God all along, but differently than Megan. God speaks into Pete's life through his intuition.

Pete is a Knower.

UNDERSTANDING THE KNOWER

Knowers are the most misunderstood of the four Prophetic Personalities, because their way of listening to God doesn't always feel tangible. They can't say, as the others do, "I heard" or "I saw" or "I felt." God's way of speaking to Knowers doesn't involve their physical senses or emotions. Knowers don't typically have visions and dreams. They don't hear God speak in full sentences. They don't routinely feel God's tangible presence.

Before Knowers learn how God speaks to them, most believe they don't hear God's voice. They read their Bible and grow in their faith. They experience the power of truth in their lives like everyone else. But when Knowers look around and see others having clear interactions with God, many question the authenticity of their own experience.

If you're a Knower, you might feel like an unspiritual person.

What It's Like Being a Knower

- God speaks to **KNOWERS** through intuition, wisdom, and clarity.
- **KNOWERS** receive the voice of God through a strong but undefined sense.
- **KNOWERS** have a spiritual sensitivity distinct from their emotions and physical senses.
- A **KNOWER'S** faith life is rooted in instinct rather than in feeling or thinking.
- **KNOWERS** are as spiritual as anyone else but might worry they are not.
- **KNOWERS** can't always explain how they know; they just do.
- **KNOWERS** lead with clarity, conviction, and wisdom.
- **KNOWERS** often know the best way forward.
- **KNOWERS** are commonly right about the way something will turn out.
- **KNOWERS** possess an internal lightbulb that illuminates "aha moments."
- When **KNOWERS** ask God, they immediately receive clear direction.
- Other people often seek out **KNOWERS** for their wise insights.

You hunger for God and His voice, but when you enter spiritual environments, you may not really feel like you belong. You can't remember a time when you used the phrase "God said this" or "God showed me that." If someone were to try to pinpoint how you hear God speak, you'd have to admit that He gives you more of an intuitive sense than a tangible feeling. The impressions He gives you do not involve your emotions. You might even feel personally detached from them.

To an outsider, Knowers seem to lack proof they can hear God's voice, but evidence has nothing to do with reality. God's method of speaking to Knowers involves supernatural perception, intuition, and wisdom.

Put more simply: If you're a Knower, God speaks to you in your "knower"—some call it spiritual insight or inner knowing. Others think it's just good old-fashioned common sense. But as a Knower, you know in your spiritual gut when God is speaking to you, and you respond to Him.

Merriam-Webster defines *intuition* as "the act or process of coming to direct knowledge or certainty without reasoning or inferring."[1] When your Prophetic Personality is a Knower, you have a *supernatural* intuition. What's the difference between the two? The source! When our intuition is rooted in the Holy Spirit rather than our own understanding (Prov. 3:5–6), He can work in ways that surpass our senses and intellect. His words to us bring peace even if we don't have an explanation for them.

I wholeheartedly believe that knowing is a clear and evident way He speaks to some of us. But due to the nuanced nature of their connection to God, an entire group of people in our faith communities has never been acknowledged as Knowers. Consider this your stepping-out party!

BIBLICAL KNOWERS

Some of you might be thinking at this point, *Havilah, show me this Knower thing in the Bible. I'm not fully convinced.* Okay, let's go there.

Intuition might not sound like a spiritual word, and it gets a bad rap in some Christian circles, but the Bible uses it. "Who gives intuition to the heart and instinct to the mind?" the Lord asked Job, being rhetorical (38:36 NLT). God does, of course.

Want to see how this works in the Bible?

- Joseph's knowing not only interpreted Pharaoh's dreams but also showed Egypt how to survive during the future famine by storing the grain during the good years (Gen. 41).
- Elisha's knowing had him compel the Israelites to dig ditches to capture the water the Lord miraculously provided (2 Kings 3).
- Paul's knowing could have helped a ship full of people avoid a life-threatening situation—if only the officers had listened. Though they didn't, Paul's additional knowing saved lives (Acts 27).

Let's look at other examples, starting with Jesus Himself, the perfect representation of how to be human while living on earth. Jesus functioned with supernatural knowledge. "But Jesus, knowing their thoughts, said, 'Why do you think evil in your hearts?'" (Matt. 9:4 NKJV).

The word for *knowing* here means "perceiving." Jesus perceived their thoughts. There's a huge difference between automatically knowing someone's thoughts, like a mind reader, and perceiving one's thoughts. Simply, it's the difference between knowing *by seeing and taking in through our senses* and knowing *from perception.*

Reading someone's mind is a purely divine ability, but perceiving is a supernatural intuition.

There's no way around it: God gives some individuals a supernatural intuition. In her excellent article defending mothers' intuition, Christina Dronen helps readers understand the biblical basis for it. She refers to the work of biblical scholar Samuel Marten and his book *Thy Rod and Thy Staff They Comfort Me Book III*, where he unpacks Jeremiah 17:10. "I, the LORD, search the heart, I test the mind, even to give every man according to his ways, according to the fruit of his doings" (NKJV).

Christina writes:

> This word for mind translated in the Hebrew is literally "kidneys." A more literal modern translation could be "I the LORD search the heart and examine the gut . . ." The Jewish culture at the time believed that the gut or kidney area, more specifically, was the source of thought.
>
> Interestingly the King James Version translates this word for kidney as "reins"—as in the Latin for kidneys, renes. So it translates the above verse, "I the Lord search the heart, I try the reins, even to give every man according to his ways, and according to the fruit of his doings."
>
> Together with the heart (feelings), the gut in Hebrew refers to all the inward parts of a person. In fact, according to Martin's research, the ancients also believe the soul resided there, in the mid-driff [sic] area.[2]

In Acts 16, we see God's impression on the apostle Paul through knowing. Paul selected Timothy to be his traveling companion. Paul intuited Timothy was the right choice. We are told that Paul chose

Timothy partly because he "wanted Timothy to accompany him" (v. 3). A holy intuition—a gut-level feeling—directed this want. Clearly Paul made the right decision by following his inner knowing.

LIGHTBULB MOMENTS

After miraculous provision made it possible to build a certain church, the pastor looked back on the process and told me, "I knew it didn't make sense when we started the project. There was no way we could pull it off financially. But I felt deep down God was going to work it out. In the beginning, God gave me a knowing, which gave me the confidence to keep moving forward. I just knew deep down it was going to happen. I know that my knowing was God speaking to me. Now I look for that unique knowing as His voice."

If you're a Knower, you'll often experience similar lightbulb moments. You'll be going about your day, and suddenly something clicks. Your inner voice, the Holy Spirit, lights up your mind and heart and you think, *I'm supposed to do this*, or *I need to call that person*, or *This is the answer to that problem/situation*. You might have a sudden aha moment or a clear thought such as, *I believe God wants me to do this*. It's just that simple. You just know that you know.

Knowers' inner narrative sounds like, *I don't know how I know, but this is the right thing to do. I just know it!* Your thoughts might be, *I don't know why, but this is the right house for me*, or *I don't know why, but you're the right person for me*.

Sometimes God serves up clarity to Knowers along with a strong side dish of urgency. A specific time frame might accompany your strong sense of what to do.

As you begin to step out in your knowing, your knowledge grows in confidence through repetition. Sometimes your confidence will run contrary to your circumstances. And though you might not initially have direct evidence of what is right, facts later confirm your knowing, just as they did for the pastor who stood before his completed church.

Sometimes God serves up clarity to Knowers along with a strong side dish of urgency.

Though Knowers don't process God's messages through their emotions, their divine knowing gives them a sense of great joy, deep sorrow, compassion, and strength.

UNIQUE WISDOM

Keith told me,

I've always been good with finances. I grew up with an entrepreneurial dad who started numerous businesses. He knew how to invest. How to make money. So, when I came into my faith, I had a pretty good understanding of how to create and grow wealth. But something shifted in me as I began to walk with God. I would begin to make a financial decision, and something entirely opposite to what my mind knew to be best would emerge in my gut. I would sense a strong urge to do something else. It wasn't something I could really explain. Oh man, my business partner would be so frustrated and confused. I didn't ignore my knowledge, but I started looking for that inner leading. I started to identify it more and more frequently. I know it was supernatural because we started to experience phenomenal breakthroughs in our business. In fact, my business partner saw this happen so many times that now before we make decisions he stops to ask if I have a strong sense of what we should do.

Get this: as a Knower, when you are actively listening to God's voice, you have access to an extraordinary gift of wisdom. You will often know things that many around you will never know. Why? Because God is the One who knows things that no one else knows and sees things that no one else can see.

> GOD gives out Wisdom free,
>> is plainspoken in Knowledge and Understanding.
> He's a rich mine of Common Sense for those who live well,
>> a personal bodyguard to the candid and sincere.
> He keeps his eye on all who live honestly,
>> and pays special attention to his loyally committed ones.
>
> (PROV. 2:6–8 MSG)

You grow in your ability to listen to God in your spiritual gut. Knowing God and what He says is the beginning of wisdom. Without His inner leading, good ideas might be all you have.

God's wisdom is different from worldly knowledge (1 Cor. 12:8). "God's wisdom is not the wisdom of the world, because it can't be bought, it can't be studied for, or earned," writes artist Ilse Kleyn of her painting *The Spirit of Wisdom*. "There are many highly intelligent men who have exhaustive knowledge of the world's wisdom but are completely ignorant of God's wisdom, His Thoughts, and His Word. Job 32:9 [NKJV] says, 'Great men are not always wise. . . .'"[3]

Think of it this way: There are so many doors in your life. So many choices. And you don't know which door is the right one to walk through.

- Knowledge is the key.
- Wisdom knows how the key works.
- God tells you which door to open and when to walk through it.

Here's another way of putting it: Knowledge gathers facts. Wisdom knows when and how to apply those facts to a specific situation. God's voice is the wisdom available to the Knower about any given situation.

In his landmark book *The Pursuit of God*, theologian A. W. Tozer wrote, "Why do some persons 'find' God in a way that others do not? . . . The one vital quality that they all had in common was spiritual receptivity. Something in them was open to heaven, something which urged them Godward."[4]

The more you hear the voice of God in your life, the more easily you'll be able to identify and step into the divine purpose God created for you. He wants to use you as an instrument in His hands to help fulfill this purpose.

HONOR YOUR KNOWING

A few years ago one of my sons burst through the door after a long day at school. Nothing seemed out of the ordinary at first. I started making him food, because the number one love language of my sons is food. (Boys aren't complicated. If they're unhappy, it's usually because they need a basic need met: food, sleep, being outside, physical contact, and so on.) The moment he walked past me, I felt an urgent need to talk to him. I asked him if he'd be willing to talk after his meal. (This might be my greatest tip of the whole book: Let a man eat before you ask him to go deep. *Eat before deep.* You're welcome!) He agreed.

Soon enough, we sat on my bed. I began to ask him some probing questions. At first he was shut down. "Mom, why are you asking me this stuff? What do you want?" I wasn't getting anywhere, and honestly, I didn't know where I was trying to go. So I did something I rarely do. I looked at him and said, "Sweetheart, I felt like the Lord wanted me to talk to you. I don't know what's going on, but I felt like there's something you need to share with me. You're not in trouble with me, and if you don't want to share, you don't have to, but God interrupted me because He's concerned about you."

His frustration melted. His eyes filled with tears. He opened up and told me about some kids that had been picking on him. He didn't know what to do.

We talked for a long time. It was possibly one of the deepest heart-to-hearts we've ever had. But if I had ignored my inner knowing, I would've never known the heavy weight he was carrying in his heart. My knowing has become my secret parenting skill.

Knowers have a unique ability to be aware of things that other people are not aware of, and to take note of events as they are happening. This type of connection to God is an on-the-job experience. You receive an impression or conviction directly from God, in the moment. You rely on this spiritual insight, understanding that it's connected to what He wants you to do or to say, because God gives you this guidance not only for yourself but also for others.

Kevin explains: "People often consult me on interpersonal issues because of my gut instinct. My instinct on a lot of stuff is usually right. I can also read between the lines and know the root of what they're saying."

If you don't pay attention to your inner knowing or heed God's prompting, you—and perhaps others—might miss the most important things God wants you to know.

There's nothing more heartbreaking for me than meeting a Knower on the road or at a book-signing line and hearing him or her say things like, "But I knew I shouldn't have married him . . ." or "God told me to, but I didn't listen." These words are always accompanied by pain and tears. Dismissing your inner knowing can lead to years of regret and pain.

If you are a Knower, I want to grab you by the shoulders and look you straight in the eye. I want to remind you that the voice of God is there to love and protect you. To remind you that you should stop everything you're doing whenever you feel Him nudge your supernatural intuition.

> **Dismissing your inner knowing can lead to years of regret and pain.**

Then do what you know you should do.

Break up with the romantic partner.

Stop hanging out with those people you call "friends."

Resist rescuing the person who doesn't want to be rescued.

Talk to that stranger you just passed.

I want to pull you close and say, "Please pay attention. Whatever God wants you to do will be worth the temporary discomfort. Don't exchange that for a lifetime of pain."

Here's your perfect ending as a Knower:

- **STOP** believing the lie that you're not spiritual and don't hear God's voice.
- **START** actively honoring your supernatural knowing and intuition. Believe God speaks to you.
- **GET BUSY** using the unique wisdom and supernatural knowledge you've received.
- **SERVE OTHERS** by putting your knowing into action in ways you are uniquely qualified to do.
- **SHOW UP** in life as a Knower!

DISCOVER YOUR TYPE

[God] communicates with us through the avenues of
our minds, our wills and our emotions. The continuous
and unembarrassed interchange of love and thought
between God and the souls of the redeemed men and
women is the throbbing heart of New Testament religion.

–A. W. TOZER

"OKAY, SO WHAT WOULD YOU SAY YOUR PRIMARY
Prophetic Personality is: hearing, seeing, feeling, or knowing?"

I was asking my brother-in-law, Daniel, as we sat on the couch
in his living room one morning with coffee in hand. He thought
about it for a moment. "I would say . . . well, it's hard because I can
point to times when God has shown up for me all four ways. When
I'm ministering to or prophesying over somebody, I pay attention
to all of them."

I hear versions of this answer all the time.

Everyone who follows Christ can receive messages from God

through the Prophetic Personalities. Like Daniel, a person can get these messages in all four ways, but most people find they lean toward one type over the others. You can think of this like a learning style: just about anyone can learn through visual, auditory, tactile, or experiential methods, but most people find they learn best through a "primary" approach. The next four chapters of the book will get into how you can mature your *primary* Prophetic Personality. Don't skip the other chapters, as they'll have valuable insights for you. And if you skipped any previous chapters, you might want to revisit those. You might be surprised to recognize how active your secondary or tertiary Prophetic Personality is.

I want to pause here for a second to talk about prophecy to those readers who might be unfamiliar with it. Prophecy is one of the spiritual gifts—along with others such as wisdom, great faith, and healing—that the apostle Paul mentioned in 1 Corinthians 12:

> There are different kinds of spiritual gifts, but the same Spirit is the source of them all. . . . A spiritual gift is given to each of us so we can help each other. . . . He gives one person the power to perform miracles, and another the ability to prophesy. He gives someone else the ability to discern whether a message is from the Spirit of God or from another spirit. . . . It is the one and only Spirit who distributes all these gifts. He alone decides which gift each person should have. (vv. 4, 7, 10–11 NLT)

Sometimes the messages you receive are for you, and sometimes they are for others. When they are for others, whether that be one person or a whole nation, they are called a prophecy.

Remember how I first defined Prophetic Personality back in chapter 3? Here it is again, with one addition:

PROPHETIC: How *God* shows up in your world
PERSONALITY: How *you* show up in your world
PROPHECY: How God shows up *through* you *to* the world

When God shows up, it is always for our benefit and the benefit of others, because He loves us so much. Even "hard" words and discipline are for our good. And words that seem to be just for us— such as the vision Britney got to open a café—touch the lives of others. Trust God to make it clear in each instance whether the word He speaks to you is for yourself or is to be offered to someone else.

If I asked you the same question I asked Daniel, you might give me a blank look. Maybe you feel like you straddle two types, or even feel thinly spread among all four. If that's the case, I would say, "You're broken!"

I'm kidding.

There's absolutely nothing wrong with you.

WHY IT'S A GOOD IDEA TO IDENTIFY YOUR PRIMARY TYPE

Your Prophetic Personality validates your uniqueness and identity. It reveals the extraordinary way God created you and speaks to you. You aren't just a face in the crowd to Him. He knows every hair on your head (Matt. 10:30). He formed you in your mother's womb, proving He's an active and engaged Creator (Ps. 139:13–16).

You aren't just a face in the crowd to Him.

Your Prophetic Personality is God's primary way of speaking

love and direction into your life. It's one thing to hear that someone loves you, but it's another to listen directly from their lips. It's your secret communication. Once you know it, you experience it everywhere. Your encounters with God expand from every once in a while to day by day. You experience Him as an up close and personal God.

Knowing your Prophetic Personality helps cut through the confusion and gives you a specific identity. Once you see it, you can't unsee it. When you know what it is, you don't shut down how God can speak to you but become more in tune with the way you best perceive His voice. This supports your living in a connected and authentic relationship with God. Anything becomes possible. You pay better attention. You learn more. You become more effective. And that's where things get powerful!

For some of you, bells and whistles and fireworks went off in your head as you read one of the preceding chapters. You instantly identified your primary method for perceiving God. It was uber clear. If that didn't happen for you, if you feel uncertain or maybe even confused, this chapter is for you.

The first thing to do, of course, is go to God and ask Him for discernment about your Prophetic Personality type. What does He want you to know about the way He communicates with you? What does He want to confirm in your life? Expect Him to give you an answer as you remain open to receiving His voice.

QUESTIONS TO HELP YOU ASSESS YOUR PRIMARY TYPE

I asked Daniel another question.

"Okay, I'm sure you experience God in all four ways, but I want you to think about how He speaks to you *personally*, when no one else is communicating to you on His behalf, and you're not communicating His words to others. You're just paying attention. What's the main way He speaks to you?"

Daniel made a case for two or three of the categories, but nothing seemed to click.

"Let's look at it a different way," I said. "When you bought your house, how did you know it was the right house to buy? Did you see yourself living here, or did God say something to you about it when you walked in?"

He paused, clearly scrolling back in his memory to that moment. He finally said, "Well, I would say I just knew it. I just walked into this house and immediately felt a sense of peace. It was the house for us."

We talked about a few other key moments in my brother-in-law's life. How did God confirm he was to marry my sister? How did God direct him to his career? His answers revealed a similar pattern. In most cases Daniel just knew.

"So maybe you're a Knower?" I asked.

He answered enthusiastically. "Yeah, I guess so. I'm a Knower!"

When it's hard to figure out your primary Prophetic Personality, ask yourself these questions:

1. How does God speak *to* me (rather than *through* me)?

It's easy to get confused about your primary personality when you're focused solely on what speaks to others and your impact on them rather than how God personally interacts with you. During a church service when the pastor urged everyone to pray for a person seated next to them, Tom prayed for a woman he'd never met before. Though Tom's primary Prophetic Personality is Hearer, during that prayer God gave him an image. When he described it to the woman, he learned he was describing a scene from a story she had published years ago. In his day-to-day life Tom usually hears words and phrases from God. But that night God gave him a vision just for the woman who sat next to him.

2. How did God speak to me at the beginning of our relationship?

God got your attention at the start of your faith life, but how? What encounters did you have with Him that caused you to believe He was real? Examine those early experiences through the lens of Prophetic Personalities. Maybe you were overwhelmed with the magnitude of His love, relieved beyond measure to receive the gift of His mercy. Maybe you're a Feeler.

3. Have I focused so much on how God speaks to others that I've allowed myself to be discouraged?

If you worship in an environment that elevates a specific type of spiritual gift, be aware of the comparisons you make. If the church reveres Gabe because he hears God's encouraging word for the church body every Sunday, or if everyone seeks out Grace because she always has a cool vision about their lives, but someone just questioned your knowing because they couldn't verify it . . . you might feel a tad invalidated! But trying to be something or someone else won't change who you are. Nothing beats genuine honesty. Lean into God and ask Him to guide you into His will for you. He won't disappoint.

At this point you might still think you have multiple primary types. It *is* possible that you're bilingual. Or trilingual. Or . . . quadrilingual (I may have looked that up)—you regularly experience

God through all four types of communication. But encountering the types isn't the only evidence you can use to identify your primary Prophetic Personality.

Let's keep going.

4. What has hurt me most deeply?

Jessica had a tough time figuring out her Prophetic Personality.

We sat in the green room at her church, deep in conversation. I asked Jessica the first three questions to discover her type, but nothing seemed to click. I asked if she'd be willing to tell me more about her story.

We landed on her love life.

She took me back just a few years to an excruciating moment of heartbreak. Jess was a well-loved single woman who had grown up in the church and served on staff for a few years. Not one to casually date, she trusted God to bring the right man into her life. She waited for years.

One Sunday morning a newcomer named Brandon visited the church. He quickly became a regular and won over all her favorite people. Moving in the same circles, Jess and Brandon became acquaintances, then friends, then inseparable friends. Soon Brandon was hired to the church staff.

Jessica was having feelings for Brandon but never breathed a word to anyone.

One day a man she highly respected for hearing God speak called her on the phone. He asked permission to share something with her that he felt was from the Lord. She agreed.

"Jess, I can't shake it. I was praying, and I saw a picture of you and Brandon together, and you were married." Stunned, Jessica accepted his words but kept them private after their conversation.

She anticipated God was doing something supernatural. She'd never uttered her feelings aloud, so how would this man know her deepest desire?

But she also felt confused. Brandon and Jessica had never talked about marriage or even dating at that point. She didn't put it past God to do something miraculous though. So she continued to get closer to Brandon and believed in the picture she had received.

Days turned into weeks, then months. A year later, nothing had happened.

Well, something happened. Jessica heard from a friend that Brandon was dating someone. But what could she do? Brandon had never suggested he thought he and Jess might be together someday. Still, she was heartbroken.

As Jessica recounted this experience, her devastation was clear. Brandon eventually married the girl he was dating. Jessica stayed on staff, having a front-row seat to Brandon's developing relationship. Jess said the most confusing part was the confirmations along the way that Brandon would be her future spouse.

I asked her what was most painful about this experience. She said, "When that man shared the picture with me, I could see it! It was as if the moment he shared it, I was instantly filled with faith for it to happen. It was going to happen. I just knew it!" (Before judging Jess, understand that creating fantastic love stories is in our nature. Don't believe me? Have you ever seen *Sleepless in Seattle*? Rom-coms set us up all the time!)

This specific situation was so painful for Jessica because it was connected to her primary Prophetic Personality type. She received a picture that lit up her faith! Jessica is a Seer.

The things that bring you the most pain often point to the unique way you experience life. What hurts you most can be a clue to your Prophetic Personality. Work your way back to painful episodes and ask why they were so damaging to you.

If you've experienced the most pain in feeling left out of spiritual things, maybe you're a Knower. Have you been devastated by your emotions? It could be evidence you're a Feeler. If you've had big dreams that feel impossible to explain and might

The things that bring you the most pain often point to the unique way you experience life.

even have been dashed, maybe you're a Seer. If you've ever felt used or exploited for your spiritual perception, perhaps you're a Hearer.

5. What do I need most from God?

Identifying what you are looking for also reflects how God created you and gives you direct evidence of your Prophetic Personality.

- Are you looking for a feeling of being loved and connected? You might be a Feeler.
- Are you looking for more confidence and clarity? You might be a Knower.
- Are you looking for an open conversation so you can ask Him questions? You might be a Hearer.
- Are you looking for a vision or a clear picture of your future? You might be a Seer.

6. How do I communicate God to others?

As I mentioned previously, you might not always receive and express in the same way. But if you're still uncertain, consider that your primary way of expressing God to others might hint at how you best perceive Him. If you want others to experience God in their emotions, that might point to you being a Feeler. If you want them to know the truth, it might mean you're a Knower. You get the idea!

STILL CONFUSED?

Discovering a primary personality type is the most difficult for these two groups of people:

1. Those who have been communicating with God for a long time. It's hard to say which way makes you feel most connected because you simply accept that God speaks to you.
2. Those who have been disconnected from God for a long time. You no longer recognize what connects you to Him.

If you belong to one of those groups, go back to question number two and spend as much time as you can reflecting on your experience of falling in love with God (even if those of you in group two wonder if that experience was real). What was that like? How did God impress on you a desire to be with Him? As you recall these moments, you'll gain insight into your primary type.

If you're still unsure, add the following two strategies to your questions.

First, ask someone close to you for their observations. "When I talk about God, what phrase do I use the most? *I know, I feel, I heard,* or *I saw*?" It's not a sure indicator, but it can provide some external perspective. If they don't know, ask if you can talk about your first encounter with God, or a painful experience you had, and see if you can pinpoint your type together.

Also make note of your experiences this week, especially any moments in which you were aware of God. Write down as much as you can. Did a particular song speak to you? Did someone say something to you about God that stuck with you? What about a passage from a sermon, your Bible reading, or even a social media post? Make note of what speaks to you in those moments. Ask yourself whether God is using one approach more than others to reach you.

And finally, if you are still doubtful, visit my website at https://truthtotable.com/free-quiz/ to play a quick game of Twenty Questions (really, there are only twenty to answer) and get my take on which Prophetic Personality you are.

THE MOST IMPORTANT THING

No matter how clearly or accurately you feel you can pinpoint your Prophetic Personality, here's what I want you to know: At various points in your walk with God, you'll experience each of the types. Familiarizing yourself with each one will help you catch *more* of what God is speaking to you and to others. You'll have greater insight into things such as why your best friend always feels something spiritual going on, or why your mom always seems so intuitively wise (even if she doesn't know it).

As you get to know each personality type, you can work on expanding them in your life. Even though you probably have a dominant mode, learning about all of them gives you a chance to develop them further.

When you understand how God communicates with you, it helps you become more effective in serving His purposes. The key is to understand how God made you and to make the most of your strengths. "Getting it" can make a huge difference in how you live your life and pursue your goals. It's all about embracing who you are and trusting He made you as He did *on purpose*.

Now let's explore the keys to developing your Prophetic Personality!

NURTURING YOUR PRIMARY PERSONALITY

DEVELOP THE HEARER

I will hear [with expectant hope] what God the LORD will say,
For He will speak peace to His people, to His godly ones.

–PSALM 85:8 AMP

DID YOU EVER HEAR ABOUT THE YOUNG MAN WHO WAS
sitting in his mother's hair salon when he caught one of her clients
watching him? "I have a prophecy for you!" she told him. She asked
someone for a piece of paper, and she wrote the message on it. "Boy,
you are going to travel the world and speak to millions of people."

This "boy" was in the process of flunking out of college, so
he wasn't too sure about that. But she wrote her name on it—Ruth
Green—and the date: 1975.[1]

A few months later, he decided to become an actor. He was
good at acting. In fact, he was exceptional. He developed his talent
and became one of the most recognized actors of our time. You
may know him as Denzel Washington, an Oscar-winning actor

who has indeed had many opportunities to travel and speak to millions.

"What she told me that day has stayed with me," he said in an interview. "I've been protected. I've been directed. . . . I didn't always stick with [God], but he always stuck with me."[2]

You see, some little old lady living her best Hearer life shared the words she had received, even without a guarantee that they would change the course of this man's life. Wow!

Hearers, what a big and powerful skill you have been given! You're the conversationalists among us. You have so many words in your life. Some you say, others you hear, but you're constantly communicating with God.

It's as if you're wearing a Bluetooth speaker in one ear so you can hear the signal coming through from heaven while the other ear is free to listen to what's happening around you.

He shares. You share.

You have a dialogue with God and offer it to others. You can speak to world leaders, history-makers, and the next generation's greatest voices. Wouldn't it be awesome if you could get a message from God to them (before their bodyguards threaten to take you out back)?

Think long and hard about these questions:

- What could God do through your life because you can hear Him?
- What messages are direct assignments God has given you to give to others?
- Who's waiting for you to bring them a message of hope?

My friend Lauren once told me this story:

When my husband and I first married, we lived in a certain house for about a year and a half. It was summertime, and I remember sitting on the back patio one morning, drinking some coffee. I was having my little conversations with God. Out of the blue I said to Him, "Hey, is there anything coming up that I should know about?"

That was my question, and I literally heard Him say, *You're not going to be living here very long.* Which was weird because we had just renewed our lease. Well, within four or five weeks our landlord called us and said, "Hey, I know you guys just signed this lease, but I'm wondering if you'd be interested in getting out of it early. I'd really like to sell the home."

It was crazy; I thought, *Really?* But I immediately recalled what God had said. Had I heard God speak to me? Yes! I had. *Oh my gosh,* I thought. *That's so wild.*

I love it! God knows I like a good plan. No, that doesn't happen all the time, but when I'm talking with Him, I get words, I hear words, literal words. Hearing is dominant for me.

We know that God is everywhere, and anyone can hear His voice. But it's often hard to listen to Him, especially in a busy world. As a Hearer you tend to excel at hearing *clearly* what God wants you to hear. Because you have this skill, sometimes God gives you words to share with others who can't hear as clearly: "Yes, He says He loves you, Margaret!"

Let's summarize the traits that characterize a Hearer: God shows up in your world as a Hearer through words. He uses phrases, sentences, conversations, and stories to speak to you. You encounter the voice of God through a play-by-play experience. You're the one who can pinpoint what you heard God say, when He said it, and how it affected you.

STRENGTHS OF A HEALER

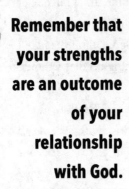

Remember that your strengths are an outcome of your relationship with God.

I'm going to say this of every Prophetic Personality: Remember that your strengths are an outcome of your relationship with God. They don't create your relationship, but they are supernatural benefits of a healthy and intimate relationship with your Creator. Here are some of the things that make Hearers exceptional.

Hearers have a unique ability to hear the voice and thoughts of God.

As a Hearer you have a supernatural way of hearing God's voice with exceptional clarity. You aren't trying to put a picture or a feeling into words. You already have the words, phrases, and conversations God shares with you. The language is unambiguous. It's clear. It cuts through the confusion and brings clarity to anyone who hears.

You hear what others can't seem to hear. Not everyone hears God as you do. Being a Hearer is a beautiful thing! Your perception of His voice is also distinctive from the voice and perceptions of others, so you find it easy to trust in Him. Mature Hearers are so familiar with His voice that they recognize it effortlessly. You have constant conversations with God, sharing your heart with Him, and Him sharing with you.

Kevin explains it this way:

I hear God's voice. I don't mean I hear a booming, commanding voice that commands me to do stuff. I mean that I hear God as a whisper in my heart and mind. It's as if He's whispering His words into my spirit.

Sometimes the words are so clear and profound that I can write them down on paper. They're often way too profound or unexpected for me to have come up with them on my own—it's like someone else wrote them for me. They're not just random thoughts either; sometimes the words are about things happening in my life right now or things that will happen in my future.

When I hear these things from God, it feels like a special connection between us because we're talking directly through our spirits. He's communicating with me directly through His Spirit instead of using someone else to tell me what He's saying— that's why it feels so personal!

God's voice is different from yours. When you hear Him speak to you, it's not like you're having a conversation with yourself—it's more like having a conversation with someone who knows everything about you and can see the future. That sounds scary, but God never intends to hurt us or make us feel bad. He loves us so much that He wants what is best for us, even if it means we must do something difficult or change our lives somehow.

"Call to me and I will answer you," God promises, "and tell you great and unsearchable things you do not know" (Jer. 33:3).

Sarah explained it to me like this: "When I hear God's voice, it usually comes as an idea or thought that seems too smart for me to have come up with on my own. I often get these creative thoughts that would come only from God, so if it directs me toward a good outcome, even if I don't like it, I know it comes from Him."

Hearers can point to the specific moments when they heard God.

You can expressly point to a moment of hearing that grounded your confidence. You remember the moment His words filled your heart and mind. You can recount the time and place He encountered you.

Moses had such an extraordinary encounter with God at Mount Sinai (Ex. 19). You have had similar encounters with God. Even if they weren't on a big mountain or introduced by a burning bush (Ex. 3). Your interactions can be much more subtle. Maybe it happened on a trip to Target. While wandering the aisles, you walked by a book and God said, *You're going to write a book one day.* Maybe it happened during your morning devotions, and God told you something to tell your friend. It felt urgent, but you didn't know why. It might have taken place on your summer trip when you were fourteen, sitting in the backseat of your parents' minivan. You heard a clear message. You didn't know how or when, but you can't dismiss what you heard. It was real! And now you live with an inner narrative that sounds like, *God said it; I know when He said it. I believe it even if I can't see it yet!*

Here's a supercool characteristic of a Hearer: when you share the things God has given you, the act of sharing grounds you in the reality of God, and it also grounds others.

Hearers can independently receive and protect the word they've heard from God.

When you receive a message from the Holy Spirit, it's yours! It's also your job as a Hearer to carry out the word with courage and resolve. Hearers are strong and independent. I'm not talking about your personality—the way you carry yourself and interact with others. I'm pointing to the strength and independence already inside you, revealing your resolve and clarity of purpose. When you hear from God, you know what you've heard from His mouth and that's all you need.

You don't need to ask anyone else what they think about a topic. You don't have to read every blog post on the internet or watch every YouTube video. You have a word from God that was loud enough to hear clearly.

You know how to keep the word you've heard safe. You don't need anyone else to do this for you; you've heard it, and that's enough. "Whoever is of God and belongs to Him hears [the truth of] God's words" (John 8:47 AMP). You have the confidence to hold that truth close, make decisions based on what you heard, and let it guide your life in a way nothing else can.

"I hear God as a voice in my head," Kathy once told me. "This makes it super easy most of the time to have conversations with Him throughout my day and when I'm taking time out to spend alone with Him. Having a conversation with God is one of my favorite things. It's powerful because no one can take that word from me. It's an incredible feeling only when we fully trust the One who speaks."

Your choice to be single-minded and determined in your hearing will change your life and create a positive ripple effect in the lives of others. Let me explain: When you hear from God, His word does not just stay inside your head. It goes beyond that—it penetrates your heart and changes you on the inside! It will cause you to do things differently, and others will notice these changes in how you act, treat them, and treat others.

The word will change you from the inside out.

Hearers can document their history of God speaking and reveal it at the right time.

Part of protecting the words God gives you means writing them down somewhere you can easily refer to them, such as a journal or notebook. After you write down the word, keep it until God releases you to act on it or share it at the appropriate moment. This can be difficult because you might feel an urgency to get up and do something with your revelation just because you're excited about it. I get it! But holding the word is just as important as sharing it and acting on it.

Do you remember when God showed up and shocked an unwed, virgin teenage girl in the middle of the night with the message that she was going to be a mom (Luke 1:26–38)? Her pregnancy would be confusing to the world initially, but it would be supernatural and sovereign, jaw-dropping and world-changing.

Can you even imagine trying to sleep after a moment like that? But this girl—Mary, the mother of Jesus—didn't go public with the news on Instagram. She kept her secret until she arrived safely at her cousin Elizabeth's house, where she would be safe from anyone who might want to stone her for being pregnant out of wedlock regardless of what "God said"! All was revealed in God's perfect time, and her encounter with God is documented forever in God's Word.

So if you're a Hearer, you may need to learn to shut up! (Don't get mad at me—I'm just the messenger.) If we prematurely rush into action, we can miss out on what God wants us to learn from an experience and how He wants us to apply His word in our lives. Take time alone with God by reading the Bible and praying. Ask Him to confirm His word to you through the Scriptures or prayerful conversation with Him. Trust Him to tell you when, if ever, to reveal something He's told you.

Hearers can break open the barrier between the visible and invisible worlds.

People look to you for advice and help because you hear things from the mouth of God. God will let you know when to share what you hear with others.

There are moments when I've communicated specific words that God has given me. When I'm preaching, writing a particular part in a book, or having a conversation after a meeting, I can pinpoint what I hear God saying. If I'm brave enough to share it, the word often lands in the hearts of those listening and creates a crack from the visible world to the invisible one—the natural to the supernatural. The more I share, the more fear, anxiety, and unbelief shatter. The power of God's word can break open hearts. A supernatural sunbeam shines hope into the dark places.

As Isaiah the prophet shared, "Then your light will break out like the dawn, and your healing (restoration, new life) will quickly spring forth; your righteousness will go before you [leading you to peace and prosperity], the glory of the LORD will be your rear guard" (Isa. 58:8 AMP).

WEAKNESSES OF A HEARER

At your best you hear the voice of God precisely and can convey the most relevant points to those who need God's word. You have a unique way of hearing what others can't seem to hear. At your worst you don't think you are hearing from God, so you ignore what you're hearing or rationalize it away.

Hearers can't always see the big picture because they get stuck in the details.

Sometimes as a Hearer you can get so caught up with all the hearing you're doing, you forget that while you hear clearly, you might not hear *everything*. We can hear only as much as God wants to reveal. This is where humility comes in. If you're constantly sharing your words and messages from God as if you have the whole picture, you might miss what God is really saying. So collect and cherish those words like the puzzle pieces that they are.

Paul reminded us, "For now [in this time of imperfection] we see in a mirror dimly [a blurred reflection, a riddle, an enigma], but then [when the time of perfection comes we will see reality] face to face. Now I know in part [just in fragments], but then I will know fully, just as I have been fully known [by God]" (1 Cor. 13:12 AMP).

Hearers usually are very good at gathering the words and thoughts of God and getting all the details right. But Hearers don't always understand enough about what they're hearing to put it all together. Which means you're vulnerable to obsessing over the details.

I'm saying, "You can get stuck in the details, Doug!"

Think of it this way: If you're trying to focus on what God is saying, trying to get your thoughts out, trying to listen for clues about other people who might be present or involved—even if you're just trying to relax and have a good time with God, details can be annoying. Overwhelming.

Even more challenging is if you're not careful, obsessing over details can make you feel confused. And if you're confused, you lose, because we know God is not the author of confusion (1 Cor. 14:33). So stay humble. Collect details but don't let the details dictate or dominate.

Hearers can overwhelm people with the whole play-by-play instead of the main point.

The upside of being a Hearer is that you hear God a lot, but the downside is that you hear God a lot! You have a constant inflow of information. It's great for your personal relationship with God, but it's not great for anyone listening to you two talk. Imagine having your best friend on the speakerphone while you have all kinds of conversations with your spouse. At first, they might lean in, interested in how you're communicating. But after a while this would be exhausting, emotionally draining, and probably a little boring.

As messengers we can cloud the message, because sometimes we overwhelm those who are listening in. A certain level of play-by-play and enthusiasm about what God is saying is just too much for others to take in and absorb! No matter how charismatic you are, no one wants to be on your permanent speakerphone.

Ask God to help you pinpoint the most important elements of what He wants you to share. Nail the theme. Grab the central idea and stay focused on that message. If you keep saying, "God said, and then God said . . . and then God said, God said, God said, God said . . ." some people will start to tune out. (Have you ever failed to hear the siren of an emergency vehicle until it's right on top of you? It's like that. The sound has become so common we stop listening for it.) Some will begin to see you as the guy who cried wolf. *What's going on here?* they might think. *Did He really say all this?* Precious things (gold, red diamonds, words from God) are rare. When you learn to hone the message and share the important ones, everyone will lean in to listen.

Hearers tend to be independent and value what they've heard over what others are sensing.

As a Hearer, you most often hear God speak independently. Though your independence is a strength, it can work against you. It can lead to a lack of team thinking. You'll assume, "I heard what God said, and I'm clear! I got the word of the Lord! Just follow me!"

Like the guy in charge of a team day at your local amusement park, you'll be stuck yelling from the front, "Over here! We're riding this ride first!" only to look over your shoulder and see confusion or even frustration in those who are with you. You hear from the back of the crowd, "Team Day isn't *Me* Day!"

You might be susceptible to dismissing someone else's hearing since it didn't come in a phrase like "Thus says the Lord" or "God told me with words—like, actual words!" Be careful not to assume that what you have heard is more valuable than what others are seeing, feeling, or sensing from God. The way others perceive God is just as important and valuable. I hope this book is helping you see this!

No matter your intention, independence can isolate you. It doesn't help everyone move forward. You may assume your particular hearing style looks like leadership, but it's not the only way to lead.

Hearers often benefit from involving others in what they know God is doing. Involving others can help you to see the big picture from many different angles.

HOW TO MATURE AS A HEARER

Document your hearing with journals, voice memos, and even sticky notes.

The best way to develop your hearing is to cultivate a system of recording what you have heard. Your job is to steward the gift of hearing through documentation. Use journals, notebooks, voice memos, typed records—anything that will help you write down and recall exactly what God said.

Habakkuk 2:2 says, "Then the LORD replied: 'Write down the

revelation and make it plain on tablets so that a herald may run with it.'"

The power of writing things down will become obvious in your life. When others try to remember what God said to them through you, you can easily refer to what you wrote down. You'll have the clarity to communicate, "God said this exact thing at this exact time!"

If you're a Hearer, you may find you need to buy journals in bulk!

Build your faith by regularly revisiting what you have documented.

After writing it down, there's another step. Don't forget to go back and read this record again and again. Reading it for yourself will always build your faith. The Word promises us this truth in Romans. "So faith comes from hearing [what is told], and what is heard comes by the [preaching of the] message concerning Christ" (10:17 AMP).

For decades our pastor at Bethel Church has stewarded the words God has given him. He's compiled every prophetic word he's been given, personally and corporately, in a binder. He reads them repeatedly throughout the year. Recalling God's words helps build his faith and helps him know what to pray for.

When you take God seriously, you write down and read what God has said to you. God will respond by speaking more to those who honor and steward His words.

Don't be surprised if you begin to see God move specifically in relation to what you've been reading and rereading. There's power in declaring God's promises. It's amazing!

Write selected words on index cards and place these where you will see them often. This is another way you can remind yourself of what He has spoken to you.

Invite the Lord to speak throughout the day.

Work on saying to the Lord throughout your day, "Speak, Lord, I'm listening."

Have it under your breath. Every morning before you do anything, "Speak, Lord, Your servant is listening," and then take a moment to listen.

God will speak to you if you ask Him to. But you must stop and listen. Listening is a skill you can develop just like any other. It's something you can get better at through practice.

Ask God for clarity on what to share with whom, and when.

Wisdom knows the difference between when you should be hearing and when you should be sharing. If you want to pair your hearing with discernment for a powerful one-two punch, then follow God's lead. Being discerning can mean a few things, but I would explain it this way: using God's wisdom to figure out what's best, especially when what's best isn't obvious.

Wisdom knows the difference between when you should be hearing and when you should be sharing.

In the context of hearing from God, using discernment means asking Him to show you the right timing for sharing what He has said. It also means asking Him to remove any obstacles, such as pride, that might prevent you from exercising His wisdom. Ask Him for help and He will help you. It's that simple!

Practice building trust with those around you.

It's important to share what you've heard with others. I have found that having someone else pray with me and talk through what I've heard is a huge help in understanding what God has said. Find a friend or family member who will pray with you and listen as you explain what God has put on your heart. Then if the word is simple, such as *Eat more vegetables*, go do it! But if it's something significant, such as, *I want you to leave nursing school and start an online business*, wait until God confirms His direction through others who can safely process the word with you.

Don't force what you hear on others or demand that they hear you out. Share something, then wait. See if they ask to hear more. Be patient and wait for God's timing. As much as you might want to share right away, sometimes God asks you to wait until later when it's needed most—and sometimes you'll discover you're not supposed to share because the word was meant just for you.

God may have you convey what He has said to a specific person or a specific group of people. Maybe to your family, your staff, or your community. So patiently wait for God to give you the go-ahead. Remember, trust takes time. God tests you to see if you are trustworthy, and so do those around you. There's no rush! Having trust is worth the wait.

A Letter to Our Heralding Hearers,

We need you! We love that God speaks to you through words and phrases. How lacking our world would be if Hearers didn't continually hear the conversations of heaven. Keep learning to hear God speak to you in your hearing. Continue to document the words and stories God is giving you. The work will be worth it.

Imagine all the lives affected because you, as a Hearer, have communicated the mind of Christ to them. You courageously give supernatural words to the natural world. It's powerful! Thank you for sharing with us and revealing the story God is writing in you and us.

Thank you for repeatedly investing in your hearing to reveal more of God to each of us. We're so thankful God speaks to you in this way!

Love,
The Body of Christ

The Hearer Cheat Sheet

STRENGTHS

- **HEARERS** work independently and protect the words that they've heard.
- **HEARERS** can pinpoint when and where they heard God, which grounds them.
- **HEARERS** have a keen sense of knowing when God is speaking.
- The more **HEARERS** obey God's voice, the greater their anointing to live in the gift.
- When the word is activated in **HEARERS**, they become unstoppable.

WEAKNESSES

- **HEARERS** can't always see details of the big picture.
- **HEARERS** can sometimes cloud the message with too much information.
- **HEARERS** can tend to be independent and lack team thinking.
- **HEARERS** need to remember not to elevate their hearing over what others perceive.

MATURITY

- Honor what you are hearing and help others pinpoint what God is highlighting.
- Develop the discipline of recording and reviewing all words you receive.

- Learn to say, "Speak for your servant is listening" (1 Sam. 3:9–10) throughout your day.
- Practice building trust with those around you.
- Don't force your hearing on others.
- Seek discernment from God about when and with whom to share.

DEVELOP THE SEER

"And it shall come to pass afterward, that I will pour out my spirit on all flesh; your sons and your daughters shall prophesy, your old men shall dream dreams, and your young men shall see visions."

–JOEL 2:28 RSV

HAVE YOU EVER PLAYED THE GAME SLUG BUG?

It was a big thing in America during my childhood. The rules are simple. While riding in the car, if someone spots a Volkswagen Beetle, they yell, "*Slug Bug!*" then turn to the person closest to them and slug them in the arm. Exciting, right? My sister and I passed the time on long road trips looking for this model of car so we could punch each other. Don't forget, these were the days before devices, so we had to improvise. Without fail, once we started looking for them, we'd always see *so* many Bugs.

Here's something that really surprised me after all my research on Prophetic Personalities: Most Seers didn't know they were Seers, but once they "saw it," they realized they'd been seeing their whole life. They just hadn't known what it was!

Here's another way to think of it: Until someone tells you what you're looking for, you won't see it. But afterward you'll see it everywhere.

"When I was little, I used to have funny dreams," Jenna once opened up to me. "One time, I dreamed a classmate had terrible breath. The next day in school, he did! Other dreams were straight-forward: I would dream about the color of clothing someone wore, places we sat for lunch and what we talked about, then I'd watch it all happen the following day. It was like God was getting my atten-tion and showing me how He wanted to connect with me! It made me feel so special to Him."

Why would God communicate with Jenna about such small details? Why would He even care about these things? To think of the almighty God spending time drawing our attention to someone's breath or the color of someone's clothes sounds ridiculous. Why would He waste His divine time?

Think about it this way: Conversations between people who care about each other are about more than the big things in life. Intimate dialogue includes small and insignificant things. In a relationship, *what* you share isn't the only value. *How* you share, by connecting and continuously communicating, matters.

God wants a relationship with you. He wants to be more than a once-in-a-lifetime encounter. If you want God to be an audible voice followed by thunder and lightning, you might be disappointed. Sure, that would get your attention (not to mention make a fantastic story), but would it help you get to know God?

Are meaningful relationships healthiest at a distance? No, the closer the better when it comes to strong bonds. Having a relationship with God is the same way. He doesn't want to be known by you from a distance. He wants to be known up close and personal. He wants to speak with you in the best way for you, so you can deepen the connection with Him throughout your whole life. The prophet Joel reminded us that He sometimes does this through visions and dreams (2:28).

Jenna continued, "Another way I've learned to hear from God was by asking Him questions such as, 'God, what do You see when You see me?' Sitting and openly waiting for this answer, I often will see a picture. He will use the image to describe who I am to Him. In one instance He showed me a picture of the moon shining at night above the ocean waters. He told me that I was the reflection of Him in the water and that I looked like Him and carried His beauty but was creatively different. I saw myself through God's eyes, which forever changed how I saw myself!"

God has a personality, just as you do. Your personality includes your thoughts, feelings, and desires. God also has thoughts, feelings, and desires to share with you. If you are a Seer, understanding this side of God might be your first awareness that He has been speaking to you your whole life. Start expecting to see Him everywhere!

STRENGTHS OF A SEER

This is a chorus for every chapter: Remember that your strengths are an outcome of your relationship with God. They don't create your relationship but are supernatural benefits of a healthy and intimate bond with your Creator. Here are some of the things that make Seers exceptional.

Seers see more than most people see.

A Seer's greatest strength is seeing what God sees, often before anyone else does. God gives Seers images that are full, vivid, and often complete. He also provides long-distance vision, which allows Seers to see a destination. It's fantastic! You clearly understand what God is showing you and where He may be leading.

Sometimes God shows you an image of your future. Sometimes the glimpse is for others. You supernaturally see past all the obstacles—especially the "I can'ts," "I won'ts," or "I shouldn'ts"—with a faith that says, "But it's possible. I've seen it!"

You are full of faith that the impossible can happen. You have a clear vision of what God is seeing. You are ready to build it, create it, or share it. You have faith for the invisible to become visible.

Seers have a vision that empowers them to take risks.

You are a risk-taker. You're willing to take significant risks for the sake of the vision, whether this means sharing your vision with others or moving toward its fulfillment. You understand there's a cost, but you're willing to pay it.

You embody the encouragement of Joshua: "Have I not commanded you? Be strong and courageous! Do not be terrified or dismayed (intimidated), for the LORD your God is with you wherever you go" (Josh. 1:9 AMP).

As a Seer you are willing to step out into uncertainty because you are sure of what you saw.

Your refusal to hesitate in the face of unanswered questions is one of the more powerful things about you. As a Seer you are willing to step out into uncertainty because you are sure of what you saw. You may know only some of the details, but your vision propels you forward. You understand that if you ever want to see it accomplished, you must move. You bravely push on, knowing the vision is worth it. You can't ignore what you've already seen.

God entrusts Seers with big dreams.

God divinely designed your mind to dream with Him. Your dreams reveal what heaven sees and what God is dreaming—big dreams that would intimidate anyone else. Through these dreams Seers become the motivators who can adapt, innovate, and make it happen. Being the first to believe God can do what He said He wants you to do is a powerful strength.

Sometimes the big dream comes to you in little pieces, but that's okay. God does this so you don't get overwhelmed. Can you imagine what might have happened to Joseph if God had shown him his whole future rather than simple dreams of wheat and stars bowing down to him (Gen. 37)?

God designed you with imagination and the ability to see what is possible. Why? Here are three things I can point to right away:

- He created you to use your imagination to find creative ways to reach your world.
- He created you to dream so you could envision another way of living, sparking hope. Dreams can help dig you out of life's darkest pits.
- He created you to dream up stories of redemption, epic moments that inspire others to join you on the journey of life.

Seers' visions spark faith in the impossible.

When God shows you an image, you have faith for it to happen. This doesn't mean you don't hesitate. I mean, raise your hand if you have faith and doubt happening at the same time. Yeah, me too! But don't let your fear stop you. If you genuinely believe you're onto something unique and your seeing can save lives, cause people joy, or solve a terrible problem, then go big with your plans.

Sometimes your dreams scare you because if you were to say them aloud, they would seem crazy. You don't have all the answers or the details. But you saw enough to spark a belief in the supernatural.

Seers are undaunted by mistakes and setbacks. You understand it's all part of growth. You have great faith in what God can do with a substantial gift of wisdom and encouragement. As your faith grows, you develop the tenacity to stick with the vision for the long haul. I love that about you! Your vision is part of your legacy as a Seer.

You start with a seed of faith and a picture of what you are growing. Seers see purpose in what God wants to do. Think about your brothers—Noah, who built an ark before he ever saw rain, and Abraham, who led a nation to a land he'd never seen.

You adopt the attitude of Jesus, who "looked at them and said, 'With people [as far as it depends on them] it is impossible, but with God all things are possible'" (Matt. 19:26 AMP).

WEAKNESSES OF A SEER

At your best you see God's heart and have faith that He will accomplish His will in the world. You have a unique way of seeing what will be. At your worst you can become impatient with people and processes.

Seers have a hard time when others don't see what they see.

It's essential to recognize that not everyone has your ability to see, nor will they see visions like yours. You might have a hard time being patient with those who resist passion and express skepticism.

"What am I doing?" you explain for the hundredth time. "Well, I just told you. Do I need to clarify again?"

They reply, "We can't quite see it."

You fire back, "Well, you might lack faith."

They respond, "No, we just can't see it."

You might feel like the people who are supposed to believe you are poking holes in your boat. Their curious questions sound like challenges. "Is there really any value in building that there?" or "Why are you going there?" You might think they've sucked all the oxygen out of the room. "That sounds good, but how are you going to pay for it?"

But here's the hard truth: *They didn't see it.* You did.

I'm sure Moses had difficulty explaining what a bush that's on fire but isn't burning *looks* like. And can you imagine their questions after he came down the mountain with the Ten Commandments? Then he dragged the entire nation of Israel through the desert to a place none of them had ever seen before! Moses understood the success of his mission required him to get others to buy into it. So does yours.

From time to time you'll have to pull your metaphorical car to the curb, park it, and take a moment to remind all the passengers that the destination will be worth it. Maybe they don't lack faith, but you're a little short on patience. Humble yourself and lovingly explain the vision again. Use your God-given vision to see past human flaws and affirm the unique gifting and talent that lives within each person. Remind them of why they, too, have a critical role to play in helping to bring your vision to pass. And remind them of this simple truth: we're not trusting the vision; we're trusting God.

> Trust GOD from the bottom of your heart;
>> don't try to figure out everything on your own.
> Listen for GOD's voice in everything you do, everywhere
> you go;
>> he's the one who will keep you on track.
> Don't assume that you know it all.
>> Run to GOD! Run from evil!
>
> (PROV. 3:5–7 MSG)

Seers can focus so hard on the future that they grow weary of the present.

In the beginning Seers have a ton of enthusiasm. Dreaming with God feels like an adventure. You don't have all the details figured out, but you're going on a road trip with your big Daddy in the sky! The car is loaded, the devices charged, and the snacks packed. You've thoroughly researched your destination, and it's going to be incredible! You can just imagine arriving at your destination. You're flinging the door open, hopping out of the car, and yelling, "I'll put on my swimsuit and meet you at the pool!"

But as time passes, you realize nothing like that is going to happen.

You can grow tired while waiting—even if you're active and busy—for the vision to come to pass. Daydreams can feel like they are morphing into nightmares. The road trip never ends. You keep thinking, *Surely we're getting close*, only to encounter one more turn in the road, one more mountain to climb. You might even think, *Should I have even taken this trip? I thought God said,* I'm sending you to Paris, France! *But maybe He said,* I'm sending you to Paris … Arkansas.

Here's where the rubber meets the road: don't forget to enjoy the journey.

Heck yeah, God's dreams are inspiring! You may imagine a future unlike any you've ever known. But the danger comes when we get too attached to the destination and take our eyes off the path. Worrying about whether you'll ever realize your dreams just taints the whole experience.

So what can you do along the way? Healthy Seers turn their focus toward enjoying the journey. Even better, they focus on becoming the person they will need to be when they arrive.

If God has given you a vision in which you're married to the love of your life, working side by side and spending a long and happy life together, sitting at home on the weekends watching wedding shows might help plan your wedding, but it isn't going to help you to get and stay married. Tend to what you can influence and maybe even control. Read a book on healthy relationships to find out what contributions you can make to a strong marriage. Take your successfully married friend out to lunch and ask her for wisdom and advice. Work on becoming the best version of the person God made you to be. That's what it looks like to make investments in your dream even before it comes to pass.

Maybe you have a vision from God to launch your own business. But every time you start to make plans, your school loans slap you down. Don't roll over in defeat. Ask God, "What step can I take today?" The process, even more than the outcome, can benefit you. Every choice you make is a vote toward your future.

Seers can become disillusioned.

Being in this game for the long haul, Seers are at risk of growing weary. If you get tired enough, you can find yourself in a deep, dark season. You're so tired of holding the dream you become disillusioned; that is, "having lost faith or trust in something once viewed as good or valuable."[1] As a Seer you lose faith in the middle because the vision no longer seems beneficial.

How does this happen?

1. You tried to carry your vision alone.

Living like this can be isolating and painful. You may be strong and independent, but that doesn't mean you don't need help. The weight of a big dream is impossible to bear solo. This doesn't make you weak; it makes you human. Listen, you would have stopped the whole production for Noah if you saw him trying to build the ark on his own.

"Suzie, get my tools!"

"Noah, what are you doing?"

"You can't save the whole planet on your own."

"Let me help!"

> **God might have given you the vision, but He never intended you to carry it by yourself.**

God might have given you the vision, but He never intended you to carry it by yourself. Part of being a healthy Seer is learning how to ask for help, build a team, and develop a sustainable long-term plan.

2. You thought you'd fulfill every one of your dreams in your lifetime.

Yes, God will fulfill the dreams that He's put in your heart. But periodically He may give you a dream that will be fulfilled in the next generation. God is saying, *I'm giving your kids a dream to fulfill.*

Sometimes your dreams will happen in your generation and sometimes through your legacy. Chances are, you have a role to play in getting things started.

Just because a journey is hard and long doesn't mean you're going in the wrong direction. The apostle Paul, who took honest-to-goodness long journeys as he helped build up the early church, understood the risks of fatigue. "Let us not grow weary or become discouraged in doing good," he wrote, "for at the proper time we will reap, if we do not give in" (Gal. 6:9 AMP).

Seers can struggle with day-to-day responsibilities.

Seers often need help with the daily hustle of life. You want to change the world and save every orphan—but you can't get the dishes done. You want to write a book but have difficulty responding to emails.

Finding a will to do the daily work is an apparent disconnect for the Seer. I get it. I'm the same way. I can tell you about my Big Bad Supernatural Dream in vivid detail but struggle to get out of bed on time. Frankly, it's discouraging—discouraging enough that I've done a lot of research on this. All that research has led me to two truths: I'm not broken. And you're not broken.

This tension is the underbelly of being a Seer. Because the picture God has spoken to you requires so much faith and visualization, it requires a ton of effort and energy. But acting only in the future isn't what God wants you to do. As hard as it may be, we need to tend to the little things that are in alignment with His big dreams. Sometimes this means we can surround ourselves with people who can help us get it all done. But at other times there's nothing to do but get the small stuff done. "Whoever can be trusted with very little can also be trusted with much," Jesus said (Luke 16:10).

To manage your project's finances, you'll need to tend to your personal budget.

To encourage the masses, you need to learn how to encourage individuals.

To avail yourself of divine appointments, you need to return phone calls that might seem unimportant.

To reach the future, you must act in the present.

HOW TO MATURE AS A SEER

Write down what you see.

The advice I give to Hearers also applies to Seers. You need to write down your visions. I'm using the word *need* because I mean it! Each Prophetic Personality benefits from writing God's messages to them, but it's *critical* for Seers. Why? Because often there's quite a distance between your vision and the finish line, and it's going to take a while to reach your destination. Writing down the vision will help you to hold on to it.

Write it down! Write it in big block letters on your bathroom mirror in a dry-erase marker or your cheapest lipstick! Create a journal dedicated to your dreams and visions. Keep it by your bed or with your Bible so you have it at the ready when God speaks to you.

In addition to writing words, Seers can benefit from creating a vision board, which is a poster-size (or bigger!) collection of images, materials, scriptures, and so on that form an important visual reminder of your dream.

Write the vision but also the practical steps to get there.

Earlier in the book I mentioned the instruction from Habakkuk 2:2. I love the Message paraphrase of it: "And then GOD answered:

'Write this. Write what you see. Write it out in big block letters so that it can be read on the run.'"

Seers are often tasked with the responsibility of leading others to the vision. Together you run toward the goal. Are you all running in step with each other? Do you spend a lot of time saying the same things over and over, explaining where you are going, what needs to be done, and why?

Habakkuk was saying, "Write down the vision but make sure it's clear. When you bring others on board, they can come up to speed fast."

Get precise about your core values and priorities. As best you can, answer the key questions about your vision—what, why, who, where, when, and how—and keep up with your journaling and writing as God reveals the answers to you.

What if you don't know how to get where you're going?

Ask a buddy.

Ask someone to help hold you accountable to the vision.

Let's face it: most of us can't stay on track all by ourselves. That's why it's essential to find a coach or a small group to check in with from time to time who will make sure you're heading in the right direction. Here's a fun fact: when you have an accountability buddy or team, your chances of reaching your goals go *way* up.[2] So find your squad and get ready to crush those goals.

A few years ago the Lord said to me: *Havilah, you may have the heart to go and build and travel and speak and do the things you're dreaming. But if you can't maintain your physical strength, you'll be limited.* It was true. I had to look at my exercise habits. My sleeping. My nutrition. It wasn't always easy to know how to stay on top of these things.

Though Seers have clarity on what they want to do, sometimes they struggle to know how to do it. I'm this way, but my husband loves to map out the practical side of things. He's really good at the day-to-day. He has no problem asking me hard questions.

> **Ben:** "Well, how are we going to do that?"
> **Me:** "Well, you just lack faith. Ask God."
> **Ben:** "How are you going to do that?"
> **Me:** "Okay, you're right. We need to talk about it. We
> need to look at that."
> **Ben:** "Let's look at this together."

It's so annoying! Ha! Truly, Ben's the producer in our marriage. He makes things happen because he can get me to articulate where God's taking us. Then he helps provide me with practical steps to get it done. You can't marry Ben, but find somebody like him who can do this for you. A Seer needs a good questioner.

Start here with, *What does fulfilling God's purposes look like for me?* and *Where are we going?* The answers can help you get on the same page with your partner or team. After all, it's much easier to make those dreams a reality when you're working together. Then tackle other important questions.

- How will I measure my progress?
- What does obeying God look like?
- How will I know that I'm living in support of the vision?
- What needs to change to make this happen?
- What do I need to tend to in my heart, mind, habits, and daily life?
- What do I need to change to get where I'm going?

Having at least one organizational visionary on your dream team is key. Ideally this person has strong administrative gifts and keen attention to detail. Their strengths in the hustle complement your weaknesses. This person can add value by helping to flesh out the details of the primary vision. As the main visionary you know what you're called to do, but you don't have to do it all alone.

As God leads, share your vision with people who are present in it.

It's not uncommon for Seers to recognize someone in their dreams. God often gives us images and insights for others. Write them down and meditate on why a particular person showed up in your dream. Ask God what He wants you to understand about it. With God's release and the person's permission, courageously share the dream.

I'm always surprised by how deeply moving it is to receive a dream from someone I know. Quite often their dream is related to something God has been working on with me, something the dreamer would never know if God hadn't spoken to them.

Be patient, resist disillusionment, and trust God's timeline.

You know that feeling in your gut that something big is coming your way? Well, it's there to keep you motivated and moving forward. Even if it seems like things are going slowly, don't give up hope. You can live as a defeated dreamer or a hope-filled visionary. The choice is yours. Good things are on the horizon, and you'll get there in God's perfect timing.

God is the one who gives the dream. He is the originator, the beginning, and the end. He is the One who promises to pour out His Spirit on all people (Joel 2:28). Give yourself grace and patience for the journey. Find the balance between holding on to your vision and remaining flexible enough to let it unfold in God's perfect time. Like the psalmist, I'm confident of this: "I will see the goodness of the LORD in the land of the living. Wait for the LORD; be strong and take heart and wait for the LORD" (Ps. 27:13–14).

A Letter to Our Strategic Seers,

We need you! We love that God speaks to you through pictures and dreams. How would our world be if Seers didn't see what God was doing and partner with Him? Keep learning to honor what God says to you through your seeing. Persevere until the vision God gives you is accomplished. Your commitment is worth it.

Imagine all the lives affected because you, as a Seer, pulled on your spiritual boots and started to build according to heaven's blueprints. You have brought the supernatural world and earth together. It's powerful! Thank you for sharing with us and revealing the dreams and visions God gives you.

Thank you for investing your seeing repeatedly to reveal more of God to each of us. We're so thankful God speaks to you in this way!

Love,
The Body of Christ

The Seer Cheat Sheet

STRENGTHS

- **SEERS** see the big picture, more than what most people see.
- **SEERS** have a vision that empowers them to take risks.
- God entrusts **SEERS** with big dreams.
- **SEERS** see in a way that sparks faith in the impossible.
- **SEERS** help others catch the vision.
- **SEERS** take steps to make the vision a reality.

WEAKNESSES

- **SEERS** have a hard time when others don't see what they see.
- **SEERS** can grow impatient with the present because all they see is the future.
- **SEERS** can become disillusioned.
- **SEERS** can struggle meeting day-to-day responsibilities.

MATURITY

- Write down what you see. Create a vision board.
- Identify practical steps to make the vision happen.
- Surround yourself with accountability partners.
- Build a dream team.
- Be patient and trust God's perfect timing.

ELEVEN

DEVELOP THE FEELER

"Very truly I tell you, you will weep and mourn while the world rejoices. You will grieve, but your grief will turn to joy."

–JOHN 16:20

I USED TO TALK ABOUT SEX A LOT IN CHURCH.

Okay, now that I have your attention, it's not as crazy as it sounds. I ran an organization that focused on teaching healthy sexuality. I like to say, "We were imperfectly empowering purity." Our message of hope took us worldwide, and we taught at churches, retreats, and conferences. I often took a male communicator so that we could teach different sessions, because teaching about masculinity and femininity is best done by the same sex.

On one trip to the Midwest, everything seemed normal until the halfway point. It started with a dream I had one night. The dream wasn't about the Lord. Nope. It wasn't spiritual; it was a sexual dream.

149

My dream felt so real that when I woke up, I felt guilty. The sexual encounter in my dream was not with my loving husband. In full disclosure, it was with a stranger. I know, right?!

Now before you start speculating, Ben and I have a great marriage. We both have committed to being as honest as possible with each other. Our honesty includes talking about our sexuality and even our sex dreams. The enemy likes to hide things in the dark, so bringing these things into the light gives us a better chance of disempowering them.

After waking up, I aimed to tell Ben, who was on the trip too, but as the day unfolded I completely forgot. I didn't remember until I entered the church that night. When I walked through the front door, I felt accosted by intense feelings of sensuality. I was experiencing the exact opposite spirit I wanted to convey that night. My embarrassment quickly turned to shame. Deep down I hoped no one could read my body language. All I could think was, *I'm supposed to preach about purity and here I am, the naughty preacher!*

Now listen, I have nothing against sexual feelings—remember, I have four children! But this feeling was out of the ordinary for me. When out preaching and traveling, I feel a unique grace to stay pure in my thoughts and heart. (I have other problems, but this isn't usually one of them.)

I quickly prayed under my breath, "Lord, if there's anything I'm missing, please help me," and headed backstage to pray with our team.

The other speaker, my friend Jason, opened our prayer time with this: "You guys, I don't know about you, but I have felt such a sexual spirit in the last couple of days. My dreams have been wild. My mind feels chaotic. It's just something in the atmosphere. But I know it's not mine."

I was shocked. Jason couldn't know I was dealing with the same thing. The phrase "I know it's not mine" echoed in my thoughts like a drumbeat. I knew what I was feeling wasn't mine either. I'm a church girl who's seen almost everything, but I'd never encountered anything like this. I knew I could repent or pray about disquieting sensations, but I'd never heard that I could sense someone else's battle.

Jason continued. "You see, when something comes out of nowhere, and you know it's not in your heart and you're not hiding anything, it often points to what you're picking up from others. It's important not to partner with these types of things. It's in the atmosphere."

My spiritual jaw was on my spiritual chest, and my brain kicked into overdrive. Was he saying that just because I felt something, that didn't mean it was mine? Of course! It made sense that God would bring our organization to a place where people were struggling significantly with sexual sin!

Trying to stay focused, I joined in prayer for the evening service with the others. But I continued to wonder. How many things have I picked up in the atmosphere and taken ownership of, thinking it was me? How many times have I felt helpless or ashamed? How much time have I squandered fighting battles that weren't even mine?

My life changed that night. I felt so much freedom it was almost tangible.

One of the best questions for you as a Feeler is, "Did I walk in with this, or did someone hand it to me when I walked in the door?" If the answer is, "I picked this up," then you can be confident it's not yours. You can tell your enemy, "That's not mine!" Then, if God asks you to come to the aid of someone who needs help you can provide, you can do that.

> **Routinely cleansing your heart will protect a healthy perspective so you can hear God for your benefit and others'.**

(Yes, this truth might tempt some to blame others for things that *are* theirs to own. But if your heart is pure and your motives are true, this strategy will keep you on task, specifically as a Feeler.)

Routinely cleansing your heart will protect a healthy perspective so you can hear God for your benefit and others'. So if you're going to develop as a healthy Feeler, you'll want safeguards in place.

STRENGTHS OF A FEELER

Once again, remember that your strengths are an outcome of your relationship with God. They don't create your relationship, but they're supernatural benefits of a healthy and intimate bond with your Creator. Here are some of the things that make Feelers exceptional!

Feelers have a unique ability to experience God's emotions and catch spiritual nuances others miss.

God's emotions connect to His heart and reveal how He wants to communicate His heart to the world.

I believe the woman described in Matthew 26:6–13 was a Feeler. She entered the room where Jesus and His disciples were eating, but as a woman, she was an unwelcome guest. Despite their annoyance over her interruption of the meal, she came to do one thing: express her love and devotion to Jesus.

She brought her most treasured possession—a costly perfume. She poured the perfume all over Jesus' feet. I can imagine the entire room filling with fragrance. When the men in the room saw what she was doing, they were enraged. Judas, one of Jesus' twelve disciples, said she should have sold it and spent the money on the poor. (In John 12 we learn this is because Judas was stealing from Jesus, not because he cared about the poor. Money would be the motivator for Judas's ultimate betrayal.)

Jesus didn't let the men's judgment and disgust have the final word.

"Why are you giving this woman a hard time?" He asked. "She has just done something wonderfully significant for me. You will have the poor with you every day for the rest of your lives, but not me. When she poured this perfume on my body, what she really did was anoint me for burial. You can be sure that wherever in the whole world the Message is preached, what she has just done is going to be remembered and admired" (Matt. 26:10–13 MSG).

In that time and place, this woman's compelling emotions connected straight to God's emotions. We know that what she did was a supernatural act, because Jesus said she had anointed His body for burial. No one, not even she, could have known Jesus was about to die; this happened at the end of His ministry, right before He went into Jerusalem. But she had counted the cost of walking into a room to express her emotions and found Jesus worthy of it all.

Jesus didn't tell her to get it together and return later when she was in control of herself. No, He praised her! I believe Jesus wanted the Feeler to play this important role in His story. All these men missed what God was doing right in the middle of them. They missed the moment because they didn't understand the emotions Jesus and His Father were experiencing.

Emotions are among the most intimate things we can share with others. As a Feeler, this is what makes you powerful. You catch the emotions of God and bring them into the presence of others to be witnessed and experienced. It's stunning!

Feelers lead with compassion and empathy.

Empathy is a powerful quality. It allows you to experience the emotions of someone else, making it one of the most valuable aspects of friendship. Many studies demonstrate that empathy is the most vital characteristic of a leader.[1]

As a Feeler you experience empathy and compassion straight from the heart of God. Emotions researcher Brené Brown defines *empathy* as "the most powerful tool of compassion" and "the daily practice of recognizing and accepting our shared humanity so that we treat ourselves and others with loving-kindness, and we take action in the face of suffering." This is different from pity, the "near enemy of compassion," because pity causes us to isolate the sufferer and feel separate from them.[2]

But empathy brings us closer to each other, and compassion is a characteristic of God. "The LORD is good to all; he has compassion on all he has made" (Ps. 145:9).

- God declares Himself to be compassionate (Ex. 22:27).
- Jesus expressed compassion when He wept for His friends who were grieving the death of Lazarus (John 11:33–35).
- Jesus expressed compassion for the "harassed and helpless" (and often hungry) crowds who were desperate to hear His words (Matt. 9:36; 15:32).

Compassion is one of the defining characteristics of your loving God. Your compassion is your spiritual superpower!

Feelers are attuned to others' emotions.

The strength of a Feeler is to experience the emotions of others. This is not always a distressing or uncomfortable thing, such as what I felt with the negative sexual energy moving through that conference. Through experiencing another person's emotions, God grants insight into what is happening under the surface of their lives.

Jessica told me a little bit about growing up as a Feeler. Neither of her parents were Feelers, so they were a little mystified about how to raise her. It was clear Jess was an emotional kid, and her intense expressions of feeling were a regular occurrence.

One day when Jessica was upset, her mom reached out to comfort her. When she touched Jessica's shoulder, the Lord said to her mom, *Jessica is feeling what you are feeling right now. She's not experiencing your pain, but she is feeling your emotions.* Jessica was unaware until she was older that her mom had had a difficult childhood, and the distress of those experiences cropped up from time to time. Jessica could feel it even though she didn't understand it.

The sadness of those days has passed. "Now I love being a Feeler!" Jessica told me. "I cry almost every day, but most of the time it's for good things. I'm grateful I am a Feeler, even though it made life more difficult when I was a little girl."

Feelers experience God's emotions for others, allowing others to experience God's feelings for them.

It's a divine exchange!

God knows exactly what we each need. As a Feeler, when you're attuned to what's happening within others, you can offer tears, affection, and empathy at the right time. It allows you to show others that God not only cares about them but has strong emotions for them.

You are God's container of affection, compassion, and love. Some of the people God brings across your path would never be able to access the emotions of God without you directly hearing and expressing God's voice through your feelings.

Feelers discern what's under the surface of an environment.

From a young age most Feelers can enter an environment and immediately sense its emotional undercurrents. They're especially sensitive to negative feelings. This might be because our baseline as kids is to assume everywhere we go is a safe place. You might remember walking into a store and immediately wanting to leave. Maybe it was a neighbor's house or a sleepover at a friend's house. In any case, you find it easy to get a read on any environment, even if your only evidence is an emotion.

As you age, you might notice your emotional sensitivity growing stronger. You can use the autonomy of adulthood to leave places you didn't want to be, but your emotional radar is still part of your life. This is because God wants to use your discernment to keep you and others safe, connected, and courageous.

Many years ago I went on a mission trip to China and Tibet. One of our staff members had a powerful anointing to recognize what was happening in an environment and discern what we could do about it. Often, she would bring us together and reveal what she was sensing in the atmosphere. She had supernatural wisdom to know what we should pray for and how we could best engage with what God was doing. It was compelling!

WEAKNESSES OF A FEELER

At your best, you have a direct line to God's heartbeat. You feel what God feels with authentic intensity. At your worst, you're at risk of contributing confusion rather than clarity to what God is doing.

Feelers have difficulty functioning when things don't feel right.

Some of you are nodding your head as you read that sentence. You know it's true!

One of my sons is a Feeler. As a toddler, when he needed calm or comfort it was easy to distract him or remove him from the environment. But as he's gotten older, his feelings, if left untended, can take over the whole family! It's tempting to label him as overemotional or reactive. But Ben and I recognize his moods and behaviors as those belonging to a sensitive Feeler.

As a Feeler your emotions can make you feel vulnerable. The intensity of feeling might even seem dangerous. Some Feelers stuff those emotions deep down, unaware of the insights you possess. But when those intense feelings leak out, they have the power to take down anyone in the vicinity, including yourself.

Feelers experience a vast array of feelings. Some are from God, and others are not. It takes wisdom to discern the difference. Unhealthy Feelers can have a tough time functioning when strong emotions overtake their hearts and minds. You might unwittingly mow others down with your emotions. You can be manipulative without totally understanding what you're doing or why.

Why is this harmful? Because not everyone experiences the depth of emotions that you do. Most others will see your emotions as a personal rather than divine experience, especially if they have negative effects. This can undermine your confidence that your feelings (and the feelings of others) are from God. Developing a sufficient level of self-awareness so that you can assess whether what you're feeling is honest and helpful—rather than hurtful—will serve you well.

Unhealthy Feelers are also vulnerable to letting what they feel dominate every part of life: mental, physical, and spiritual. Learn how to identify which emotions belong to you, which belong to God, and which belong to others, as well as which are directing you to intercession and which God is employing to give you discernment. See the tips in the "How to Mature as a Feeler" section on page 164. Once again, Proverbs 3:5–8 has good advice on how to do this:

> Trust in and rely confidently on the LORD with all your heart
> And do not rely on your own insight or understanding.
>
> In all your ways know and acknowledge and recognize Him,
> And He will make your paths straight and smooth
>   [removing obstacles that block your way].
>
> Do not be wise in your own eyes;
> Fear the LORD [with reverent awe and obedience] and
>   turn [entirely] away from evil.
>
> It will be health to your body [your marrow, your nerves,
>   your sinews, your muscles—all your inner parts]
> And refreshment (physical well-being) to your bones.
>
> (AMP)

Unhealthy Feelers bring confusion, not clarity.

Many years ago, while on a mission trip to Guatemala, I had an experience with a Feeler. I didn't understand what a Feeler was back then, but I know now what was happening.

While ministering in a church service, a girl on our team began sensing God wanted to do something for the women in the room. She was so compelled by what she felt, she asked our team leader if she could share it with the room. It was significant because she was young in her faith, but having heard her heart, he agreed. Standing in front of the room, with tears streaming down her face, she shared God's heart. By all evidence, she had heard God. The women started to respond wholeheartedly. Her feelings were right!

The following night we went into another meeting, and the same girl approached the team leader with something else on her heart. This time, the leader didn't discern that what the girl felt was aligned with what God was doing just then. So he gently said, "I don't think that's what God is doing right now."

This devastated her. She broke down in tears and moved to the back of the room. Her disappointment was tangible. Everyone on the team could see she was struggling, so team members began to check on her one after another. She was a mess. She'd felt so strongly that she had a word that she couldn't contain her emotions. You could see the confusion and anxiety on her face. We all knew she had the right motives and was genuinely experiencing something, but it wasn't for everyone that night; it was for her. Her emotions had led to a breakthrough the night before, but now her emotions led to disconnection and distraction. Last night: catalysts for unity. Tonight: catalysts for confusion.

Listen, you may get it wrong at first when you're learning to acknowledge yourself as a Feeler. It's not your fault! Maybe you've been labeled as overly emotional, and you interpreted your feelings as taxing to those around you. Or you might not have had permission to honor your emotions, and now it's tough to acknowledge and respect them. On the other hand, if you grew up in a home where it wasn't safe to express your feelings or your feelings were labeled irrelevant, you may have difficulty acknowledging, understanding, and respecting them.

God wants to give you a healthy balance as a Feeler. He doesn't want you to take the atmosphere down. He wants you to lift the atmosphere up—up to the reality that recognizes God's presence is available to everyone. This is why it's so important to steward your emotions as a Feeler.

Don't be discouraged if leadership doesn't give you the green light to express your emotions in a specific environment. Don't give in to disillusionment if you think your feelings are being dismissed. If God is saying it, He will get His message heard.

> "So will My word be which goes out of My mouth;
> It will not return to Me void (useless, without result),
> Without accomplishing what I desire,
> And without succeeding in the matter for which I sent it."
>
> (ISA. 55:11 AMP)

Here's something to note:

- The healthiest Feelers are the ones who stay in a community.
- The healthiest Feelers reveal their emotions to those around them.
- The healthiest Feelers don't get caught up in all-or-nothing thinking.
- The healthiest Feelers consider their feelings to be a conversation with God.
- The healthiest Feelers know God will have the conversation when He wills it.

- The healthiest Feelers are not responsible for what others feel.
- The healthiest Feelers know their emotions are not the only route God takes to communicate with them.

Feelers can overvalue their feelings and make others uncomfortable.

You might place so much value on what you sense that you leave the other Prophetic Personalities in the dust.

The first time you experience the depths of God's emotions, you will be exhilarated. You'll feel things you never felt before. An unbridled Feeler is a stallion free to run the fields of unlimited feeling.

It's beautiful, but then it gets complicated. We can collectively agree that watching an intimate moment between two people that wasn't meant for public viewing is awkward. Nothing feels more uncomfortable than being a single on an outing with a lovey-dovey couple or watching your mom and dad make out. You get the idea!

That's what your feelings feel like for those who *aren't* Feelers. Did you catch that?

Your heart is so big, and you want to include those of us around you. You're often caught up in your intimate moment with God. You think it's beautiful. You want to enter the throne room, but your spouse wants to walk into the Spaghetti Factory. The point is, for some people the expression of your emotions can be unnecessarily uncomfortable.

If you don't express your feelings in a way that accommodates this discomfort, you can inadvertently alienate people who need what you have to share with them. Remember, no Prophetic Personality is more or less spiritual than any other. It takes humility to slow down and maybe save some expressions for later. I know you feel the emotions of God, and nothing feels more authentic than crying with those who cry, mourning with those who mourn.

So ask God for discernment. Holding the reins on your emotions requires awareness, humility, and meekness.

Doesn't meekness mean weakness? Not at all. It means "strength under control." "Who is wise and understanding among you?" asked James. "Let him show by good conduct that his works are done in the meekness of wisdom" (3:13 NKJV). Meekness is an essential attribute for Feelers. Knowing you could go deep and wide with God but choosing to exercise restraint in the presence of others is not a weakness or fear of man. It's humility.

Some Feelers undervalue their feelings.

Feelers tend to be extreme in the way they *think* about their emotions. Many who don't overvalue their feelings ignore them altogether. Those who were taught that feelings are unsafe or even sinful tend to have difficulty believing that God can actually use their emotions in the process of leading them.

Micah explains:

I grew up in a home where my mom was very emotional. My dad was the opposite—logical and reserved. Growing up, I didn't want to be like my mom. She had a nervous energy that grew worse with age. So whenever I thought about emotions or feelings, I would picture my mom and dismiss them. I often said, "I'm logical, just like my dad." Then I married and began experiencing my emotions in a way I never had.

One day my wife, Kathy, said to me, "Honey, I don't think you're as unemotional as you believe. I think you have a lot of emotions that you've never been able to reveal, because emotions seem so unsafe." When she said this, I felt angry! I would invariably shut the conversation down because the idea that she considered me emotional felt ridiculous. I was nothing like my mom. Couldn't she see I didn't live chained to my feelings?

Kathy slowly continued the conversation over time. Through our talks, I became more open to the idea. Eventually I connected my rejection of all things emotional to my childhood. My mom was unhealthy in her emotions and showed me a negative example, creating in me an unhealthy belief about feelings.

One day I had a significant breakthrough. God said, *Micah, I gave you your emotions. They don't have to be a negative, manipulative, or anxious experience. Your emotions will lead you to a deeper, richer relationship with Me and those around you.*

Years later I learned I was a Feeler. The ceiling came off my spiritual life! I began to sense things as I never had before. I was the guy crying, saying, "I cannot believe I'm crying right now! Man, my twenty-year-old self would be shocked." Once I changed the negative narrative around emotions, I was free to be me.

Many Feelers relate to Micah. You might have been taught to distrust emotions as chaotic, negative, or manipulative. Sadly, this life lesson limited your ability to engage God in your emotions, leaving you believing you couldn't hear God.

Because we humans tend to let our pendulums swing, take careful stock of where you land between the extremes of overvaluing or undervaluing your feelings. Invite God to teach you how to make your emotions available to Him to use as a strength for communication with and for Him.

HOW TO MATURE AS A FEELER

Anchor yourself in truth instead of only what you feel.

Discovering how to anchor yourself in "who God is," not just "who you feel God is," will keep you safe. "I know who God is, so that will not change based on what I feel" is the mantra of a healthy Feeler.

Even if feeling is your primary Prophetic Personality, emotions are only part of the life God intended for you to live. He also wants you to know truth—not necessarily in the sense of the Knower but in this sense: "Then you will *know* the truth, and the truth will set you free" (John 8:32, emphasis added). God didn't say, "You will feel the truth, and feeling the truth will set you free." Healthy Feelers ground themselves in God's revelation of the truth.

What is truth? Your Bible is the most accurate and rock-solid thing there is. The sea of emotions is an ever-changing landscape. You're going to feel a million different things every day, and sometimes you'll find it hard to tell what's what. Trusting your feelings instead of trusting God can be tempting, but that's a mistake. God's Word is the anchor that will stabilize your emotions and give you immediate clarity.

When you spend time learning, studying, and memorizing what God has said, it will become a part of you—so much so that when you feel pulled in one direction by your feelings or another direction by someone else's words or actions, you'll have an immediate understanding as to which course is right for you.

Remember, God is not confused. He will not say anything to you that conflicts with what He has already said in His Word. If you ever doubt this, I challenge you to study what you think He said and consider whether you might have misinterpreted it.

When you pair your knowledge of the truth with the feelings

God has given you—look out, world! On their own, feelings don't change lives. What changes lives is when the Spirit and truth come together. The Spirit of truth offers an accurate revelation of God.

Instead of dismissing your feelings, ask God about them.

Instead of telling yourself, "Stop feeling this way. Get it together," start with, "God, why am I feeling this way?" It's a perfect question for a Feeler.

Remember, God is our source of wisdom, which can save us from confusion:

> If any of you lacks wisdom, you should ask God, who gives generously to all without finding fault, and it will be given to you. But when you ask, you must believe and not doubt, because the one who doubts is like a wave of the sea, blown and tossed by the wind. That person should not expect to receive anything from the Lord. Such a person is double-minded and unstable in all they do. (James 1:5–8)

Instead of shutting down, ask God, "Why do I feel overwhelmed?" or "Why do I feel emotional?" Then after asking your questions, lean in and listen. Your feelings often reveal a pathway to what God desires to do through you. If you realize what's happening is only for you, go into your prayer closet and battle for yourself.

Often your emotions are revealing something God wants to heal in your own life. If He is trying to heal you, let Him! Own responsibility for what He is showing you, repent, and hand it back to Him through prayer

Often your emotions are revealing something God wants to heal in your own life.

or repentance. Don't carry it around! You weren't created to walk around weighed down by unresolved or unhealed emotions.

Keep your heart clean.

At the beginning of this chapter I mentioned the importance of routinely examining and purifying your heart. As a Feeler, you must keep your filter (your heart) clean because everything you do comes through your heart.

Think of it this way: If your window is dirty, everything you look at will have dirt on it. Your heart is the same way. If you don't keep a clean heart, everything you do and say will have come through a bad filter.

As a Feeler you are vulnerable to giving your heart to things that can hurt you. You're prone to "heart attacks"! You can follow David's lead by praying, "Search me, God, and know my heart; test me and know my anxious thoughts. See if there is any offensive way in me, and lead me in the way everlasting" (Ps. 139:23–24). And also, "Create in me a pure heart, O God, and renew a steadfast spirit within me" (Ps. 51:10).

Embrace the power of prayer and pray until joy comes.

God created this beautiful exchange between humankind and Himself. Prayer is a conversation He initiates, allowing us to petition Him for divine intervention.

As a Feeler it's essential you understand the incredible and effective tool of prayer in your life. Prayer is a powerful partnership between you and God. It's the very origin of your power and authority.

When you feel something deeply, ask God these questions:

- Is this emotion mine, or is it something in the area?
- If it's mine, do I need to repent? Do I need to return it to You for healing?

- If it's in the area, how can I partner with You to help bring about a breakthrough?

Then keep surrendering the burden to God until He releases you with joy.

Another thing that will help you is learning to prioritize intercession—talking to God on someone's behalf—because this is a great way to release the burden of others' feelings. I talked about Feelers and intercessory prayer in chapter 6. By prioritizing it, I simply mean making prayer your go-to strategy. Remember:

> Meanwhile, the moment we get tired in the waiting, God's Spirit is right alongside helping us along. If we don't know how or what to pray, it doesn't matter. He does our praying in and for us, making prayer out of our wordless sighs, our aching groans. He knows us far better than we know ourselves, knows our pregnant condition, and keeps us present before God. That's why we can be so sure that every detail in our lives of love for God is worked into something good. (Rom. 8:26–28 MSG)

Have your feelings, but don't allow them to "have you."

It's easy to spot immature Feelers, because their emotions dominate them. They might slap a Jesus sticker on what they express, but if anyone challenges their feelings, they won't go peacefully. They're okay only when their feelings are getting all the attention.

The mark of mature Feelers is their ability to feel things intensely yet remain submitted to their community. Healthy Feelers can acknowledge their emotions, respect what they sense, ask God what He wants to do, and then act on what He says. Humility and obedience make you extremely powerful! You will be shocked at how critical a growth step this will be for your life.

Learn which feelings are yours and which are not.

Healthy Feelers know how to quickly identify which feelings are theirs and which are not. This saves them from getting stuck carrying other people's burdens or repenting for things that aren't theirs. My coteacher Jason offered insight into how to do this:

A feeling might be from you if

- it reflects something you have been dealing with or been previously aware of,
- the Holy Spirit is convicting you of a need to repent, or
- you examine your heart before God and see you are hiding something from Him.

A feeling might be from someone else if

- it arises out of the blue and catches you off guard,
- it generates confusion, or
- other people are sensing something similar.

Ask God for discernment to tell the difference.

Steward your feelings to avoid exhaustion and burnout.

Remember, Feelers are experiencing God in ways others will not always understand. If you don't steward (manage) your intense feelings, you'll become vulnerable to exhaustion and burnout. You're not broken. You're different. Recognize that what you're encountering is deep and can be highly draining if not governed. Your ability to discern what is happening around you needs acknowledgment, awareness—and also boundaries.

As a healthy Feeler, you offer your heart to feel what God feels. You give yourself space to mourn with those who mourn and cry with those who cry. Your heart breaks for the impoverished little boy wearing clothes two sizes too big and gives its attention to the person who feels invisible. Feeling a burden for the widow sitting alone in the corner. But likewise, you allow yourself to explore the gamut of jumping for joy after watching someone overcome addiction or a relationship being restored right in front of you.

Experiencing the emotions of God gives you the eyes of heaven, allowing you to encounter others not only as human beings but as children of God. What a fantastic gift!

A Letter to Our Fantastic Feelers,

We need you! What would our world be like without you showing us the heart of God? Keep listening to God speak to you through your profound emotions. Continue to develop your discernment. It will be worth all the effort.

Just for a moment, imagine all the lives affected when you stop hiding what you're sensing and courageously reveal the heart of God. It's breathtaking! Thank you for crying with us, mourning with us, then staying with us until the joy returns. Thank you for investing your heart over and over again to reveal more of God to each of us.

We're so thankful God speaks to you in this way!

Love,
The Body of Christ

The Feeler Cheat Sheet

STRENGTHS

- **FEELERS** experience God's emotions and catch spiritual nuances others miss.
- **FEELERS** lead with compassion and empathy.
- **FEELERS** are attuned to others' emotions.
- **FEELERS** help others to experience God's feelings.
- **FEELERS** discern what's under the surface of an environment.

WEAKNESSES

- **FEELERS** have difficulty functioning when things don't feel right.
- Unhealthy **FEELERS** bring confusion, not clarity.
- **FEELERS** can overvalue their feelings and make others uncomfortable.
- Some **FEELERS** can dismiss their feelings as invaluable.

MATURITY

- Anchor yourself in biblical truth instead of only what you feel.
- Instead of dismissing your feelings, ask God about them.
- Keep your heart clean.
- Embrace the power of prayer and pray until joy comes.
- Have your feelings, but don't allow them to "have you."
- Learn what's yours and what's not.
- Steward your feelings to avoid exhaustion and burnout.

DEVELOP THE KNOWER

"What no eye has seen, what no ear has heard, and what no human mind has conceived"—the things God has prepared for those who love him—these are the things God has revealed to us by his Spirit.

–1 CORINTHIANS 2:9–10

DISCOVERING I WAS A KNOWER WAS A RADICAL SHIFT for me that changed my whole life!

Remember, I was the girl raised in a church pew, where I'd sat through thousands of sermons. Christ changed my life when I decided to follow Him wholeheartedly, and realizing I could interact with Him in such a profound, supernatural way took me to another level.

I no longer sat around feeling unworthy of encountering God. I stopped feeling overlooked or forgotten by God in that big supernatural layer of the world. I quit elevating any one mode of listening to God over another and realized for the first time that God speaks to each of us in His own way.

All the years of my confusion, comparison, and discouragement fell off like heavy, clunky armor I was never meant to wear. Immediately, I felt spiritual confidence.

God was speaking to me all the time. Constantly! On the way to work I'd notice a clear thought. On my morning walk I'd sense an urge to do something or not to do something. Plain answers to complex questions presented themselves. I started using my knowing everywhere. In my preaching, in my parenting, in my marriage, and throughout my everyday life. Nothing changed—and yet everything changed.

It was as if I had been standing on a beach taking in a view that was beautiful but hazy. Then a gentle breeze came along and pushed the haze out of the way, revealing reality in breathtaking clarity. The experience transformed me! Everything that had been holding me back vanished, including bad beliefs about not being able to access God as it seemed everyone else could. Suddenly I could recognize the stunning scope of how God connects with each of His children.

Listen, I cannot overstate this. Discovering your Prophetic Personality could change your whole spiritual life overnight. Knowers, you now *know* you're not broken. God hasn't been excluding you from His gifts. You can put an end to that toxic, untrue belief.

God shows up in the Knower's world as intuition or an inner confidence in what is true. He speaks to you in your "knower." You have supernatural intuition and insights. As a Knower, you just know in your spiritual gut that God is speaking to you, and you respond to Him.

Celebrate how God created you to hear Him. Start rocking your "I'm a Knower!" T-shirt.

STRENGTHS OF A KNOWER

As I have said all along, remember that your strengths are an outcome of your relationship with God. They don't create your relationship; they are supernatural benefits of a healthy and intimate bond with your Creator. Here are some of the things that make Knowers exceptional.

Knowers have a unique ability to push through barriers and overcome anything that stands in their way.

Knowers do hard things really well. You push through obstacles and overcome them in extraordinary ways. You have a supernatural resolve to stick with what you know.

Your knowing anchors you to what God has told you, regardless of the circumstances and barriers you may face. You know how to get through difficult things. You don't give up! Tenacity is a profound grace in your life.

Meagan, a single mom with two young children, faced a difficult decision: Should she go back to school to get her master's degree while her kids were still little, knowing it would be a tough road? *Yes*, she decided. When a friend asked how she knew that this was the right path for her, Meagan explained that she didn't have a specific vision or message from God but rather a deep understanding in her heart that this was the right thing to do.

When you pair an impossible challenge with knowing that you're on the right path, you can draw deep from your well of courage, passion, or sheer determination and push forward despite the odds. You know how to stand firm, as the apostle Paul urged us to do: "Therefore, put on the complete armor of God, so that you will be able to [successfully] resist and stand your ground in the evil day [of danger], and having done everything [that the crisis demands], to stand firm [in your place, fully prepared, immovable, victorious]" (Eph. 6:13 AMP).

Knowers can have courage that inspires courage in others. Listen, if you're riding out the storm of your life, you want a Knower in the boat. Knowers will say, "Look at me. You're going to make it! I just know God's got a plan for you. You're not going to die here. Okay?"

Knowers possess a strong sense of direction.

You have a remarkable sense of direction because your faith links with your spiritual gut. Moses ventured into the wilderness not to run away from Egypt but because he believed God and knew the promised land awaited the people of Israel (Ex. 33:1). A Knower is willing to take the land but is also really good at discerning which land to take. You're the one who often says, "I just know that's our promised land, and I'm going to get it."

You know the truth of Psalm 32:8: "I will instruct you and teach you in the way you should go; I will counsel you with my loving eye on you."

Knowers are resistant to being swept away by emotion or hype.

Knowers are unlike any other Prophetic Personality in the face of adversity because God speaks to Knowers without employing the more tangible senses of hearing, seeing, or feeling. This means during periods of stress, when you're at higher risk of being misdirected, you don't have to wait for powerful sensory forces to show you the way. Knowing is available to you 24-7. Knowers have unusual stability. You live with a conviction deep inside that propels you forward.

You know that you know, and that is enough. Period.

Knowers possess an unusual degree of hope.

Profound hope accompanies the Knower because you believe God is going to come through. This hope is "an anchor for the soul, firm and secure" (Heb. 6:19).

Knowers have unusual stability, a conviction deep inside that propels you forward.

Hope is not a feeling but an expectation that something good will happen in the future. Hope is founded on evidence that the things you know to be true will also prove to be true. For example, if you've never heard of someone being healed from cancer, you wouldn't expect healing from cancer to be possible. You wouldn't hope for healing. But once you know of someone healed from cancer, you carry undeniable hope in such healing.

Biblical hope is founded on what you know about God. If you don't know anything about God, it's hard to hope He can help you in times of need. But if you've studied the Bible and come to know His voice, if you have witnessed God's power at work in your life and the lives of others, then you will expect Him to do great things.

Knowers have supernatural hope because your expectation comes from your history of paying attention to God. Your hope is grounded in knowing that if God said it, you believe it. That settles it.

WEAKNESSES OF A KNOWER

At your best, you know with unshakable certainty what is right or best. You have a unique way of discerning God's truth. At your worst, you might believe your knowing is superior to the ways other Prophetic Personalities connect with God. It will be tempting to ignore what other members of the body of Christ have to contribute to a situation.

When Knowers feel left out of spiritual experiences, they are vulnerable to disengaging from their spiritual life.

There's nothing more annoying to an unhealthy Knower than being around others who are constantly hearing, seeing, and feeling God speaking to them. To be surrounded by others who never stop telling them, "God told me this," or "God showed me that."

Knowers often wonder, *Am I the most unspiritual person in the room? I haven't felt anything. I'm just having a regular day at church.*

Other Prophetic Personalities say, "God showed me this vision, and I'm supposed to change the world by writing this book," or "The power of God came upon me, and I now know I'm supposed to move to Asia."

The Knower thinks, *Wow! How did you get that? I just know I'm supposed to wash the laundry so it doesn't smell. That's where my life is right now.*

Listen, Knowers. It's okay. I want you to keep investing in that part of you that feels mundane and unspiritual. You don't have to fake anything. You can accept that the way God communicates with you isn't typical. You can believe God is reaching out to you even when it doesn't seem like it. God knows what He's doing and why He needs to speak to you as He does.

Don't let the flashiness of others' hearing, seeing, or feeling cause you to disconnect from your knowing. I love how Paul urged us to resist this temptation: "But each one must carefully scrutinize his own work [examining his actions, attitudes, and behavior], and then he can have the personal satisfaction and inner joy of doing something commendable without comparing himself to another" (Gal. 6:4 AMP).

Rather than envy others' ways of hearing God, allow your encounters with the other Prophetic Personalities to encourage your spiritual growth and draw you closer to Him.

Knowers have a hard time valuing other modes of hearing God.

This weakness is the other side of the coin. On the one side, you might envy other Prophetic Personalities. On this side, you judge them. Because you don't often rely on sensory experiences, you can be quick to dismiss, disrespect, or disregard those who do.

Knowers sometimes judge the Feeler for seeming over-emotional. *Need a therapist?*

The Hearer keeps giving play-by-play reports. *Do we really need to know all that?*

You get distracted by what the Seer doesn't seem to see. *Your vision is great, but how can you change the world when you can't even wash your sheets?*

Not honoring others' way of listening can leave a gap in your faith walk. The gap is called *pride*, the opposite of humility. The Bible defines humility as "having a realistic view of one's importance" (Prov. 22:4 AMP). I like how Dr. Anna Schaffner puts it: "Humility is an attitude of spiritual modesty that comes from understanding our place in the larger order of things."[1] In other words, humility means not elevating your Prophetic Personality above the others.

I'm embarrassed to say this, but in my early years of leadership I used to discredit emotional females because I'm not a highly emotional person. When I saw their tears and felt their emotion, I felt manipulated. I saw how the people in the room responded to Feelers and I felt conflicted.

But as I came to understand the Prophetic Personalities, I had to stop judging the emotional believer. I began to acknowledge how God speaks to them and even through them. I called myself out for succumbing to pride, judgment, and cynicism. The body of Christ is diverse, and Knowers are part of a larger body (1 Cor. 12:18–25).

Knowers tend to overvalue their knowing and leave others behind.

Some Knowers' attitudes seem to say, "Well, since you don't know or don't have an answer, and I already know, you can sit this one out while I take care of it. If you want to come with me, fine, but try to keep up!" (Don't look around. You know who you are.)

When these Knowers get clear about what they know, they start off down the road in a flash without looking back. "I know I'm to go here, or I'm going to buy that house. I'm supposed to go now . . . build that . . . take care of business." It feels so obvious, but when they look up, they see they've left everybody behind. If you believe you're the only one in your world that God is speaking to, you can be extremely dangerous.

Proverbs 16:25 says, "There is a way that seems right to a man, but its end is the way to death" (ESV). And Proverbs 24:6 says, "In a multitude of counselors there is safety" (NKJV). Knowers can become prideful if they have a history of being proven right. Pride sounds like, "I'm the only one who knows what to do. I'm the only one who has a clear sense, so I'm going to do this with or without you."

The safest way to move forward as a Knower is to surrender to the lordship of Jesus by finding a healthy community that honors your knowing *and* holds you accountable to authority and wisdom.

Knowers can miss God's direction, because they presume to know His destination.

You're excellent at receiving God's message but can't always take it into the end zone. Why? You can miss what God is saying *now*. Because Knowers don't rely on words or feelings, you're at risk of running the ball down the field without watching the coach for direction.

God doesn't change what He's saying because He's fickle or wants to mess up the universe. He's not changing His direction; He's challenging your presumption about what He's going to do next. Sometimes He tests us, to see if we're really allowing Him to lead. Tests bring out what and who we're trusting in. Only God knows which tests we'll need to face in order to fulfill His will for our lives.

Think about Abraham. God told him to sacrifice his only son, Isaac, as an act of obedience. Then, before Abraham killed Isaac, God told him to do something else (Gen. 22:1–18).

When God says to the Knower, *I love you, but slow down, look at Me, and pay attention,* you need to stop. Knowers need to check in with God consistently and relationally. Staying close to God is the only way to stay in touch with His immediate direction.

Stay humble. Seek Him, and you will find Him again and again.

HOW TO MATURE AS A KNOWER

Develop your supernatural wisdom by leaning into the mind of Christ.

This means we honor the spiritual disciplines that keep us rooted in the Spirit. Paul wrote: "The person with the Spirit makes judgments about all things, but such a person is not subject to merely human judgments. . . . We have the mind of Christ" (1 Cor. 2:15–16). True knowing is *informed* by your intuition, but it can't be supernaturally wise if it's not also informed by spiritual maturity. Nurture your growth:

- **STUDY SCRIPTURE:** Regularly read and meditate on the Bible. Seek God's wisdom and revelation within its pages. The Word of God is a rich source of spiritual wisdom and guidance.
- **CULTIVATE A LIFE OF PRAYER:** Pray continually (1 Thess. 5:17); adopt habits that include periods of stillness and silence; and keep your heart quiet, humble, and receptive to God's revelations.
- **STAY CONNECTED TO A FAITH COMMUNITY:** Participate in a community of believers who are actively pursuing spiritual growth. Surround yourself with others who can provide mentoring, accountability, and encouragement in your spiritual journey.
- **ADOPT OTHER SPIRITUAL DISCIPLINES THAT DEEPEN YOUR CONNECTION TO GOD:** Regular practices such as fasting, worship, and solitude will keep your heart receptive to His wisdom and correction.

Allow God to build a history of knowing with you.

Unlike any other Prophetic Personality, your confidence as a Knower is critically connected to your history of listening to God. Obey God's leading and trust Him to honor your intent and correct you if you are wrong. You don't have to be perfect—just humble and willing to learn. This is how we learn the difference between natural human thinking and supernatural knowing. Repeatedly putting your intuitive sense into practice, then having it confirmed, is what leads to confidence that your knowing is accurate. You need the mileage.

Gradually accepting and eventually embracing your knowing

at the deepest level will give you confidence that you are receiving what God has to say to you.

Nurture humility so God can lead you.

Humility is the recognition that your knowing is limited. To mature as a Knower, it's crucial to cultivate humility by acknowledging you don't have all the answers, that you always have more to learn. Grow by living fully submitted to God and trusting His leading. Adopt this attitude: "God, I'm fully submitted to You. Do whatever You want to do in my life." Humility helps you to recognize that you need the wisdom of heaven. The good news is that it's always available.

Practice humility by seeking feedback from others. Engage in discussions with other Prophetic Personalities and be open to their insights and perspectives. Actively request constructive criticism, then receive it as an opportunity for growth rather than a personal attack.

Honest self-reflection can also support humility. Regularly question your assumptions and biases, presenting them to God for His assessment. (This is part of inviting Him to develop a history of knowing with you.) By embracing humility, you foster a mind-set of continuous learning and growth, which leads to maturity.

Don't believe the lie that you're not spiritual enough.

You've got to ditch that thought once and for all. Break up with that lie. Delete the number and block it! That mind-set no longer serves you.

Adopt this new mantra: "Just because I hear God differently doesn't make me wrong. It makes me different." Value your identity by acknowledging that you listen to God in a unique way, and that's okay. You may even have to say to yourself in the mirror, "Hey you, you're not going to be the one who's getting a bunch of visions, and you probably won't be using the phrase 'Thus saith the Lord' anytime soon. But that's okay because that's just not you!"

Mostly, you will have to tell yourself the truth. "I'm a Knower. I will value the fact that with the gift of knowing comes the gift of wisdom. I will build my confidence on my history with God. He has made me a Knower with supernatural intuition, and I can grow and steward my knowing!"

> **Value the fact that with the gift of knowing comes the gift of wisdom.**

Embrace discomfort.

If the previous suggestions haven't made you uncomfortable enough, here's one more: you won't mature as a Knower until you push beyond your comfort zone and actively seek discomfort. Have another look at the list of Knowers' potential weaknesses. Note how they have a common theme of separating from others and isolating, whether that's caused by overconfidence or hurt feelings. Staying engaged despite a default tendency to withdraw is going to lead you into situations you'd rather escape! Don't run away. Allow your confidence to be challenged. Explore opposing viewpoints. Engage in difficult conversations. God's got you! He won't abandon you.

Learn to articulate what you know with phrases that others are less likely to interpret as self-proclaimed.

Turning the focus off your gut and onto God will help convey what God has impressed upon you in a way others can receive and trust. Sometimes phrases such as "I think" or "I know" or "I believe" are misunderstood as coming from us rather than from the Lord. Hearers tend to say things like, "God said." Seers say, "God showed me," and Feelers say, "God moved my heart." Knowers can adopt a similar approach, such as with "God impressed on me that . . ."

It's fine to use terms familiar to other Prophetic Personalities. For example, sometimes when I'm sharing what God has given me with a Hearer I will say, "God *spoke* to me," even though God didn't use words or phrases. Or I might say to a Feeler, "I really *feel* God is . . ." If I express to Seers the *vision* God showed me, they give me their attention.

Paul wrote about the benefits of meeting others where they are in this way: "I'm *flexible, adaptable, and* able to do and be whatever is needed for all kinds of people so that *in the end* I can use every means at my disposal to offer them salvation" (1 Cor. 9:22 VOICE).

Try relating to others with this kind of openness and see what a difference it makes in your life and ministry.

A Letter to Our Knowledgeable Knowers,

We need you! We love that God speaks to you through your gut. How would our world be if it weren't for your confidence in your divine intuition? Keep learning to hear God speak to you in your knowing. Continue to develop supernatural clarity in this confused world. It will be worth it.

Because you have ceased to believe that you are not spiritual enough, your courageous willingness to reveal the mind of God will affect many lives for the better. It's powerful! Thank you for standing with us, revealing God's wisdom, and sticking with your spiritual gut.

Thank you for sharing what you know with us and not shrinking back. We're so thankful God speaks to you in this way!

Love,

The Body of Christ

The Knower Cheat Sheet

STRENGTHS

- **KNOWERS** are overcomers. They possess a unique ability to push through barriers and overcome anything that stands in the way.
- **KNOWERS** have an invaluable sense of direction.
- **KNOWERS'** stability keeps them from being swept away by emotion or hype.
- **KNOWERS** are frequently right about the way something will turn out.
- Once **KNOWERS** encounter the truth of God, little will stop them.
- **KNOWERS** grow in confidence by grounding themselves in their history of hearing God, and that confidence helps them lead with hope.

WEAKNESSES

- **KNOWERS** can feel left out and tempted to disengage from their spiritual life.
- **KNOWERS** have a hard time valuing those who hear God differently.
- **KNOWERS** tend to overvalue what they know and leave others behind.
- When God changes direction, **KNOWERS** can often miss God's leading.

MATURITY

- Allow God to establish a history of knowing with you. Be obedient and heed what you intuit He is telling you.
- Practice humility.
- Don't believe the lie that you're not spiritual enough.
- Grow in your wisdom, discernment, and intuition. Trust your spiritual gut.
- Learn to share what you're sensing by saying, "God impressed on me" instead of "I just know."

LIFELONG LISTENING

THIRTEEN

WORDS FOR US ALL

Above all else, guard your heart,
for everything you do flows from it.

—PROVERBS 4:23

GOD UNIQUELY CREATED YOU TO LISTEN TO HIM IN A
particular way, but He created all of us to communicate with Him.
When you listen to God and encounter His truth, you find freedom.
Jesus said to His disciples, "Then you will know the truth, and the
truth will set you free" (John 8:32). And when you know truth and
freedom, little can stop you from accomplishing what He has given
you to do.

As you mature, you gain confidence that comes from encountering truth firsthand. The truth grounds you at your core. You are sure
of what God said. You got it! Once you know what the biblical truth
is, you're all in. You're a force to be reckoned with. You've located the
truth, and as a result, you have extraordinary courage and resolve.

Also, your confidence in God's truth will enable you to challenge others or even to be challenged yourself. You're not afraid to do what's right because you know it's right. Popular opinion doesn't influence you. Even doubters and judges will not distract you from your hard-and-fast, rock-solid conviction. You know God is with you! He has spoken clearly. You might feel fear, but you are not confused.

You might feel fear, but you are not confused.

No matter what your Prophetic Personality is, all of us have common ground in the following truths. Remembering them keeps us anchored to God.

WE ALL NEED RELATIONSHIP WITH GOD

When I was learning how to use my knowing, it wasn't all kicks and giggles. In fact, in the beginning I noticed something that really bothered me. I heard God's voice regularly, but I wasn't growing closer to Him. I sensed I was further from Him than ever. I couldn't understand why this was happening. Wasn't I supposed to get closer to God the more I interacted with Him? I really wanted that.

One night while flying home from a speaking event, I sat in the darkness of the cabin with the sound of the humming engine filling the air. In the quiet I asked God, "Why do I feel so distant from You even though we're talking every day? It doesn't make sense. What am I missing?"

He replied, *Havilah, it's because you're having only a transactional relationship with Me, not an intimate relationship.* The truth of His words painfully hit my heart. He was right. I had never thought about it that way before.

A transactional relationship is one we invest in for the sake of getting something in return. We keep things good with our work bosses because they keep us employed and paid. We consult teachers because they give us instruction and doctors because they can point us toward health. We take care of pets because they give us a sense of well-being and maybe even purpose. When we interact with God to get special blessings or to get our way, we miss the point: we are relational beings.

God gives us our Prophetic Personality for the sake of an intimate relationship with Him. The primary purpose of an intimate relationship is to know and be known, to love and be loved. Does this mean you never get anything out of an intimate relationship? Of course not. Spouses support each other in practical ways; parents instruct children; friends give each other a hand. But intimate relationships aren't *only* transactional.

Imagine what you'd be missing if you never learned how to communicate with your Creator. What if you could never talk to your architect, the One who knows everything about you? What if you couldn't ask the questions He alone can answer? Everything you need to know, God knows. You were never created to do life alone. You need the voice of God in your everyday life.

But again, this communication isn't a one-way street. Whether through hearing, seeing, feeling, or knowing, God uses your Prophetic Personality to reveal Himself to you. For starters, because He designed them, they reveal important elements of His character:

- God hears (John 9:31; 1 John 5:14).
- God sees (Gen. 16:13; Prov. 15:3).
- God feels (Jer. 31:3; Ps. 103:13).
- God knows (Ps. 147:5; 1 John 3:20).

As you spend time with God in His Word, reading and listening in the unique way He made you, you'll discover more and more about who He is.

I'll say it one more time: one of the most important things I want you to know is that the strengths of your Prophetic Personality are the *outcome* of an intimate relationship with God. You can't nurture those strengths or mature in your listening skills apart from Him. So gently turn your heart away from the idea that God gave you a Prophetic Personality as a spiritual perk and see it for what it really is: a path to experiencing the fullness of God in a deeper way.

We all benefit from being careful not to seek our gifts more than we seek Him. When we leave this earth, we will take our relationship with the Lord with us, but we won't take our special method of listening with us. We won't need that in heaven, where the barriers of this physical world no longer exist, and we can experience God face-to-face (1 Cor. 13:12).

WE ALL NEED TIME FOR RELATIONSHIP WITH GOD

Before I married and had children, you could often find me at Starbucks with my Bible and my notes and my favorite drink as I prepared to teach at church. I'd spend whole days there, a luxurious eight hours at a time, studying God's Word and the commentaries. It was wonderful. It was holy.

I married at twenty-seven. By the time I was thirty-five, I was a mother of four and an ordained minister. I was on a teaching team, and I was preaching and traveling. When I wasn't traveling, I was teaching at a large church that held five services per weekend, and those five services were my responsibility once a month. Often I was up all night. I was tired. I tried to sit with God, I tried to study and prepare to teach, but time got shorter and shorter. I would walk into meetings with folks who'd prepped for hours, and I'd think, *I only had an hour. I just pray God will anoint it anyway!*

From time to time I'd longingly think of those long days with God at Starbucks, and I realized something important: time that I had once thought of as holy was more accurately just uninterrupted. You know what I mean? I couldn't afford the luxury of long hours of uninterrupted time with God anymore.

But the other truth is that holy moments with God are never out of reach. We often hear Him more clearly in church settings because that's when we make time to quiet our souls and look for Him. But God can just as well get our attention while we're going about our everyday life—talking with someone, driving to work, doing the dishes, walking the dog. It doesn't matter where—or when—you encounter God; what matters most is how you respond when He makes Himself known!

Moms aren't the only busy people in the world. You might work multiple jobs while supporting a family or studying for a degree (or both)! You might be an entrepreneur with a lot of ventures in development. You might have the responsibility for large numbers of employees, students, congregations, clients, aging parents, or patients.

How can we find time in the busyness of life to listen to God and develop that important intimacy with Him?

The Bible says that we are to not only listen to the Word but to do what the Word says (James 1:22). Now, let's dig a little deeper, shall we? We're not talking about just going through the motions here; we're talking about tapping into something that's uniquely ours. So let's use wisdom and creativity to navigate this, rather than blindly following some set formula. Remember: the real gold lies in how we can harness our creativity to figure out how to do what God's asking us to do, and that includes developing an intimate relationship with Him.

I once had a pattern of spending hours in the Word. When that pattern had to shift, I didn't deny or abandon my need for time with God. But I did have to rethink how to make space for it. I started subscribing to Bible-teaching podcasts that I could listen to during carpool. I discovered a phone app that would read the Bible aloud to me while I was showering (which would happen about every four days). I bought a little Bluetooth speaker that I set on a table next to the chair where I nursed my babies. Every three hours I could sit for fifteen or twenty minutes and listen to something—an encouraging word, a message—that would support my Prophetic Personality and my relationship with God. Rather than stubbornly stick to an ideal of what my time with God *must* look like, I developed new habits. Don't change the goal; change the method.

Refusing to let shame influence or overwhelm us supports our efforts to get creative as we adapt to life's demands, which are ever-changing. The Lord gave me four boys. They are my first ministry and my first congregation. God isn't asking me to lock them in a room all day while I go spend time with Him apart from them. You are not a bad believer if your faith life doesn't look exactly the way Michael's or Holly's looks, or even the way you think yours *should* look. You steward what God has given you and be realistic. I do my best with the best I can bring, and I ask God to fill in the cracks.

Here's the deal: instead of getting caught up in all the noise, let's cut straight to the chase with a question that really matters. Ask yourself, *Did I do my best?* That's the litmus test. Your best effort is

WORDS FOR US ALL

the real deal, and that's what's going to set the tone for your journey. That's what God cares about.

WE CAN ALL GROW

The Bible says we are to "produce fruit in keeping with repentance" (Matt. 3:8). The kind of fruit God wants to help us grow (Gal. 5:22–23) aren't things you can just pick up at your spiritual farmer's market. Don't you wish you could pray self-control into your life? Wouldn't that be great? But we can't. We have to grow it in our lives. We have to cultivate the habits that result in good fruit. And we do this through actively working on what matures our Prophetic Personality and our ability to listen to God's leading.

When I was developing my knowing, God was very gracious to me at every step. Listening to God was straightforward, and believe me, I asked Him *everything.* "Should I go here or there? Can I do this or that?" I mean, I asked Him everything because I was young, and I was learning. This is good. Peter wrote, "Like newborn babies, crave pure spiritual milk, so that by it you may grow up in your salvation, now that you have tasted that the Lord is good" (1 Peter 2:2–3).

Eventually you will mature in God to the point where you're eating solid food (Heb. 5:14). Over time my sons grew from needing milk every three hours to eating meat. We cut it up into bite-size pieces. Pretty soon they could cut up a big chunk and feed themselves. Now, having matured in my Prophetic Personality, I tend to sense what God is saying even before I ask Him anything. But remember what I said about spending time with God? If we don't nurture the relationship, we'll go hungry and our fruit will shrivel up.

I check in regularly, asking, "God, what are You saying to me?" I'm in the Bible consistently. We all need to be in the Bible. I don't care who you are—a pastor, a theologian, or a regular Joe Christian. The Bible is God's Word in physical form, and He is in its pages, and He speaks to us there. So we go into the Word, and we nurture our relationship with God. We feed the soil that produces good fruit.

Staying with the food metaphor, I like to say the Bible is like a pantry. When the Spirit of God wants to give you something or show you something to do, He'll pull something nourishing out of the pantry to give you fuel for the effort. If we don't stay in the Word, we can become malnourished. The cupboards are bare, and we go to God desperate: "Do You have any food? Do You have any spaghetti sauce? Do You have *anything*?" When you're in the Word regularly, your spiritual pantry will always have plenty on hand to feed you.

So if you have a hunger for God to speak to you, grow in your Prophetic Personality. Start with the suggestions in the "How to Mature" section of your type. And no matter how mature you are, continue to invest in your intimate relationship with God. Read and learn, listen, obey, and grow.

WE ALL HAVE ACCESS TO GOD'S WISDOM

If you lack wisdom, all you have to do is ask God for it (James 1:5). As you practice your Prophetic Personality and grow more skilled at recognizing and obeying His voice, God will become your direct line to wisdom, insight, and love.

Think about it. God's Word is powerful beyond measure (Heb. 4:12). It's not just Scripture, but when you pair Scripture and communication with His revelations to you, there is nothing the two of you can't do. A word from God can solve the worst marital problem. I have seen the power that one word from the Lord can have on sickness and disease. If you are in a financial crisis, the Lord can tell you how to turn your situation around. This doesn't mean God's word is a magic wand that we can wave to do our bidding. It is not a star to wish on to make all our dreams come true. It means that we have access to God's power, and when we are in relationship with Him, we also have access to His wisdom.

By aligning your mind with God's, you can learn "his good, pleasing and perfect will" for any situation you face (Rom. 12:2). When you listen to God, He will lead you in the way you should go (Isa. 48:17). Be assured that if you heed God's wisdom, He will direct your steps (Ps. 37:23–24).

WE ALL SERVE A DIVINE AUTHORITY

I never intended this book to answer every deep and theological question surrounding the voice of God. Instead, I set out to write a practical guide that helps anyone who follows God learn how to discern His voice.

That said, when I teach that everyone can hear from God, most people worry to some degree that this kind of statement opens the door to disaster. Don't I know that people can't be trusted with that kind of permission? Am I not aware that all kinds of imposters have done all sorts of things ranging from ridiculous to horrifying because "God told me to"? Even people who mean well get it wrong sometimes.

How can I teach the Prophetic Personalities without fear that terrible things will happen?

First, I trust that the God who gives us the ability to hear, see, feel, and know Him can also protect us from our own immaturity and imperfection while we learn to grow. He won't abandon us any more than I'd abandon my kids when they look to me for instructions on how to use a knife or cross the street.

Second, God has appointed authorities over us to help us test His revelations and grow in wisdom. One layer of authority is church leadership, which is why I urge everyone to become an active part of a faith community that practices listening to God with the Prophetic Personalities. When Paul met with the elders of the church at Ephesus for the last time, he admonished them to remember their responsibility to the church body:

> So guard yourselves and God's people. Feed and shepherd God's flock—his church, purchased with his own blood—over which the Holy Spirit has appointed you as leaders. I know that false teachers, like vicious wolves, will come in among you after I leave, not sparing the flock. Even some men from your own group will rise up and distort the truth in order to draw a following. (Acts 20:28–30 NLT)

Remember the Feeler from chapter 11 who believed she had something to share publicly? When she took it to her leadership for permission, she was hurt to be told that the word wasn't appropriate for that time and place. She was hurt and confused—but she was also protected.

God is not the author of confusion.

God is not the author of confusion, which means He can't contradict Himself. Anything truly from God won't run counter to the Bible. So it is our ultimate test. The Bible, not human opinion, has the final word. Discard any seeming revelation or insight that conflicts with it or you'll find yourself building your life on a foundation of deception.

WE ALL NEED COMMUNITY

If you're not already firmly rooted in a church that will support your desire to listen to God and mature in your Prophetic Personality, I strongly urge you to find a community where you can thrive. Find a place that will help you learn and follow through with whatever God is asking you to do.

You can fellowship with anybody. There are no rules against that. But being in a group that has the same desire to grow in faith will accelerate your growth. A great church is like Miracle-Gro in your spiritual soil. Look for a community committed to pursuing God, transforming hearts, and helping people fulfill their purpose as children of God. Trust me: when you walk through the doors, you'll know if the Spirit is present. You'll know if people you meet have the kind of hunger for God that Paul outlined in Romans 12: teaching, exhorting, serving, giving, prophesying, and leading with zeal and cheerfulness.

One of the great things about living in this age is that we can connect with people who aren't local. If you can't find or attend a church in your area, jump online and get support and teaching from the Spirit-filled churches who offer access to their ministries and resources. Bethel Church, where I am the women's pastor, has Bethel TV and a multilingual podcast. Search for online groups and events that support your learning. Attend conferences if you can and begin to gather a circle of friends who are like-minded in pressing into God, even if they don't share your zip code.

As with wisdom, you can ask the Lord to direct you to people who can help you—and who you can help in return. He is the God of divine appointments! Together the family of Christ is unstoppable, as it was from the earliest days of the first church:

> They devoted themselves to the apostles' teaching and to fellowship, to the breaking of bread and to prayer. Everyone was filled with awe at the many wonders and signs performed by the apostles. All the believers were together and had everything in common. They sold property and possessions to give to anyone who had need. Every day they continued to meet together in the temple courts. They broke bread in their homes and ate together with glad and sincere hearts, praising God and enjoying the favor of all the people. And the Lord added to their number daily those who were being saved. (Acts 2:42–47)

ANSWERS TO LINGERING QUESTIONS

When God speaks, he does not give new revelation about himself that contradicts what he has already revealed in Scripture. Rather, God speaks to give application of his Word to the specific circumstances in your life. When God speaks to you, he is not writing a new book of Scripture; rather, he is applying to your life what he has already said in his Word.

–HENRY T. BLACKABY

WHEN I TEACH THE PROPHETIC PERSONALITIES COURSE in person, students tend to ask the same kinds of questions over and over. Here are the most common ones.

HOW DO I KNOW WHAT I'M PERCEIVING IS FROM GOD AND NOT MYSELF?

When you're learning to develop your skills, it's important to test what you're receiving from God. How do you do that? Here's a five-step method.

1. Consult the Word of God.

In chapter 13 I talked about the Bible being our ultimate litmus test for the truth of any message. Compare what you believe God has given you to what the Bible has already said. God will never give you a word that contradicts what He has already communicated. If what you're hearing contradicts the Bible, it's not from God. The best way forward is to dismiss what you thought you heard and keep practicing. If you're not sure whether it's at odds with the Word, talk about it with your pastor or other spiritual leader.

What if what you heard isn't specifically addressed in the Bible? Go to the second step.

2. Consult the community of believers.

Share the word you've received with a godly person you trust and ask them for counsel. The Bible says there is wisdom in a multitude of advisers (Prov. 15:22). Ask them, "Does this sound like God to you?" Then trust their replies. In other words, be careful not to dismiss counsel that isn't what you want to hear. If you respect the people you have asked, even if you disagree with them, God will honor you.

Abi, a Feeler, would often get intense feelings during church worship services. In the beginning she wasn't certain whether these feelings were hers or whether they were coming from others. When this happened, she would go to someone in the same worship service—sometimes a trusted friend, sometimes a person she knew was spiritually more mature than she was—and she would ask: "What are you feeling right now? What do you sense is going on in the room?" This person's feedback would help her figure it out. Getting guidance and confirmation is one of the best benefits of being in a church: we can forge meaningful relationships with people who are wiser and smarter than we are!

What if you can't get clarity from this step either? Keep going.

3. Ask God to confirm His message.

The Holy Spirit has no problem confirming what He's saying over your life. When in doubt, ask: *Lord, would You please give me a sign that I'm hearing You correctly?* Ask in confidence that He wants you to hear Him. Remember when God told my sister Deb over and over (and over!) that she was entering a new season? God might confirm His word to you through a scripture, through a person, through a song or story, through nature, through something your preschooler says—He can use anything! Keep your eyes, ears, heart, and mind open. When God wants us to get something, He will do everything in His power to help us find it.

> **When God wants us to get something, He will do everything in His power to help us.**

4. Ask, "Does the message affirm love?"

When you get a download from God, you will be encouraged. Yes, even if God is correcting you or redirecting you, encouragement will be the prevailing effect. An encounter with God should leave you feeling like you've been hugged on the inside. You just interacted with Someone who is crazy in love with you! His love will permeate every interaction, regardless of how hard the message is.

If you experience anxiety, worry, hate, apathy, fear, or anything that is contrary to love, God is likely not the source. "For God has not given us a spirit of fear, but of power and of love and of a sound mind" (2 Tim. 1:7 NKJV).

5. Ask, "Does the message bring clarity and hope?"

When you get a message from God, you'll feel ready to act upon what you've received. You might feel a shred of hesitation, but this will be nothing compared to the hope coming to life in you. You may have felt distressed before He spoke to you, but afterward a seed of "but God makes a way" will begin to sprout in your heart. Any fog of confusion will begin to lift.

Listen for what sounds like Him, for the words that match His heart and character. God's voice will always bring clarity to confusion, a solution to a problem, or an answer to a question. He gives peace, hope, and an awareness of His presence in your life. His voice is the one that believes in you, encourages you. It reminds you that you are not alone, and a natural response could be "Thanks for that!" or "That's what I needed!" or "Wow!" or "I'm going to do that!"

As you learn to recognize how God communicates and you practice and grow in your ability to connect with Him, you'll be able to discern the source of these messages quicker and more accurately.

Testing God's Message Cheat Sheet

1. Consult the Word of God.
2. Consult your pastor, other spiritual authority, or the community of believers.
3. Ask God to confirm His message.
4. Ask, "Does the message affirm love?"
5. Ask, "Does the message bring clarity and hope?"

IS THE MESSAGE I'VE RECEIVED
FOR ME OR SOMEONE ELSE?

Feelers aren't the only ones who ask this question; you might not have an instant revelation one way or the other. Typically, if it's for you, the message will revolve around an issue you're already aware of on some level. You might have been actively seeking God's wisdom about something specific or the message might address something you're only marginally aware of. But once it presents itself, you can't deny that it's relevant.

The same principle applies when the word is for someone else: if it's for them, it will relate to something already on their minds and hearts. So if you hear, *I want you to go to work in China*, but you've never even thought of vacationing there, that word is likely for someone near you. If you say, "I think God is saying He wants you to go work in China," this will not be baffling if it's for them.

Corinne was in church when she sensed God saying, *Your children are going to be all right*. She hadn't been the least bit worried about her children, so she asked God what He meant. *Should* she be worried? She checked her phone for emergency texts or calls. Nothing. As she prayed about it, He nudged her to speak to the woman standing in front of her, a stranger. Really? Wouldn't the woman think she was rude at best, irrational at worst?

She tapped the woman's shoulder. When she turned around, Corinne was surprised to see she had been crying. This was a bad time to interrupt. Or maybe it wasn't?

"I'm so sorry if this sounds weird," she said. "I don't usually do this. Do you have children?"

"Yes, two," the woman said, and Corinne felt instant relief.

"I believe God wants me to tell you that they're going to be okay," she said. The woman shared that both of her children were in serious crises, and she had just been praying for them. Corinne's word brought her powerful comfort!

HOW TO GIVE SOMEONE A MESSAGE I'VE RECEIVED

If you believe you have a word for someone else, remember that they might have been asking God for a confirmation of His word in their lives, and God might want to use you to do that.

1. Ask them for permission to share it. "God has asked me to tell you something. May I share it with you?" or "I think I have a word for you from God. Would it be okay if I gave that to you?" This is a respectful way to invite them to willingly participate in what God is doing. You don't have to force yourself on anyone. Remember, God is a gentleman.

2. Consider submitting it to leadership first. If you believe you have a word for the room you're in, you should tell your leaders about it. God has appointed them over you for your protection as well as the congregation's. If leadership allows it, you have their authority behind you. If they don't, you can trust they're exercising God's wisdom on your behalf. Let's break this down in a way that hits home. See, your mission here is to be a true steward of that word—and that means going the distance, pushing the boundaries. Now, here's the thing: that might mean sharing it with someone directly, or it could mean passing it up the chain to those who steer the ship. But listen closely, success is all about showing up, being

present. It's not solely about dishing out that word. That's the key difference you need to grasp. Got it?

One more thing before I leave this topic: Sometimes I see a stranger and sense God's love and compassion for them, but I don't get a clear word to share. I don't feel I have anything to offer. What is the obedient thing to do in this situation? First, always ask God: *You've highlighted this person to me. What are You bringing to my attention? What do You want me to do?* Often the Lord is busy drawing somebody to Himself, and if you're in the area to assist, He'll use you! Ask God, *Should I pray with the person? Maybe just talk with them?* If His answer makes you respond with *Do I* have *to?*, the answer is . . . yes. Yes, you do.

Without making it about you and your spirituality, introduce yourself with something like, "This may sound funny, but I'm a Christian. I follow Christ. And I don't know why, but I sense that God drew my attention to you. Is there anything I can pray with you about?"

Anything can happen. I've had rejection and I've been received. What matters is that you're listening and responding to God. People don't usually refuse prayer. And often when you pray with someone, God meets them.

WHAT IF WHAT GOD SAYS TO ME CONFLICTS WITH WHAT HE SAYS TO SOMEONE ELSE?

Let's be honest: the enemy loves to bring confusion anytime he can (John 8:43–44). We've established that God is not the author of confusion. The enemy is! We don't always like to talk about the enemy.

We understand he's under our feet (Rom. 16:20), but we still have to deal with him (Eph. 6:11).

Your spouse, your business partner, your coleader—these people are not your enemy. Perhaps one of you thinks God is saying "act now" and the other hears "act later." One thinks God wants you to go; the other person says to stay. One says jump and the other says dive. One says chocolate, and the other says—it doesn't matter! *Always* go with the chocolate.

Just kidding. Sometimes, though, we have to laugh. Because we can see what's happening: the enemy wants to put up walls and open up chasms between us.

If possible, get a godly third party to help you figure things out. Maybe your pastor, a counselor, a financial adviser, a strategist—you get the picture. Start asking questions—not about who's right but about what you're trying to accomplish. Without feeling rushed, try to find the main point. Where are you trying to go? What is your objective? Are you genuinely trying to hear God or are you focused on advancing a personal agenda?

Another important consideration is what role you play in the situation's specific environment. If you are an appointed leader, you have to lead. Yes, consult your team. Listen to the voices of anyone who is affected by your leadership and take their concerns to God. Ask Him, "Are You speaking to me through them?" Sometimes the answer will be yes, sometimes no. If you were Moses and asked this of God about the Israelites, God would have said, *Yeah, some of them are pretty upset, but they don't have the big picture. You can get the lowdown from Me.* God will help you. He *will* give you clarity and confirmation.

If you are not in a leadership position, you can trust that God has appointed these leaders and holds them to a high standard.

Will there be times when God tells you that it's time for you to accomplish a different purpose than the one He has called them to do? Yes. Will you know when that is? Yes. Will you know when you need to stay even if you don't want to? Yes—if you check your ego at the door. Stay rooted in love rather than anger or offense (Eph. 3:16–19).

WHAT IF I HAVE AN UNBELIEVING SPOUSE?

Listen up, single people: the challenges this presents is one of the reasons the Bible warns us not to become "unequally yoked" with unbelievers (2 Cor. 6:14). It's hard in life and especially in marriage. There's value in falling in love with and marrying a believer.

Now, not everybody has that luxury. Some of us met God after we met our spouse. Some of our spouses have lost their faith in God. Some of us married unbelievers anyway. The best thing you can do is mature your ability to listen to what God is saying to you. Ask God to change your spouse's heart and, until that happens, to work on changing you to become the most loving demonstration of God for your spouse's benefit. Rather than pray, "God, please show them that I'm right" (even if you are), learn to pray, "God, please show them who You are."

It takes two yeses to make a yes in a marriage. When that kind of agreement isn't available to you, you have to wait for it or risk damaging the marriage. Don't undervalue your contribution to keeping peace. If you have God's word but you're a punk, that's not going to help your spouse want Jesus. Be willing to learn how to honor your spouse and yourself at the same time. It's possible. I've seen it over and over again. Trust Him for His perfect outcome.

WHAT IF I HAVE SUPPRESSED MY GIFT?

Sometimes we experience things, especially in childhood, that teach us to bury our gifts. We do this to protect ourselves. If you endured abuse, you might have conditioned your heart and mind not to feel anything, even if you are by design a Feeler. If someone punished you for hearing a voice from heaven because only crazy people hear such things, you might have started ignoring God's voice. If someone betrayed you and trampled a vision that was holy to you, why would you risk sharing your dreams with anyone? If someone told you your knowing can't be trusted because you're too sinful and stupid to know anything, maybe you believed them.

If any of this rings true to you, here's a good place to start:

1. Self-awareness is the first step. When we know what needs healing, we can expect God to heal. "He heals the broken-hearted and binds up their wounds" (Ps. 147:3). Maybe the healing will be supernatural and instant or maybe it will be slower, in which case we can accept the Lord's invitation to go on a journey of healing. When you embark, take all the time you need. There's no rush to get you healed so you can be used for God. He can use you according to your willingness and ability no matter where you are.

2. Become an active participant in your healing. Get into action mode here. It's time to tap into every single resource that's at your disposal. Look, I'm talking about going all in—connect with a Christian counselor who's got your back; jump into one of those recovery groups, whether it's at your church or out in your community. Don't hold back; reach out to your pastor and ask for that prayer support you need. And don't

overlook your physical wellness either. Go have a chat with a physician and figure out what steps you can take to heal that aspect of your life. God has equipped certain professionals to help us when we need help. This is their gift—they have committed their lives to helping people. God appoints them for our benefit just as He sent Ananias to Saul to heal his blindness (Acts 9:10–19). Saul's healing marked the beginning of his ministry as the apostle Paul, and this encounter was a gift to Ananias as well.

HOW SHOULD I DELIVER (AND RECEIVE) CORRECTIVE MESSAGES?

God has a way of sending us course-correcting messages, and looking back, I've seen a few of those blessings in disguise. Let me share a couple of thoughts on what made them real blessings for me.

First, I humbly embraced these words when I understood they were coming straight from a God who genuinely loved me and wanted to shield me from unnecessary pain. It's this belief that when these words are coming from a loving God, they're His loving discipline for our good (Heb. 12:4–11).

Now, here's the second thing: the delivery matters too. It's like a recipe for success. When those words reached me, they were wrapped in love and raw honesty without a hint of judgment.

I picked up this nugget of wisdom a little late in life, while navigating the challenges of parenting four energetic boys. See, there's a

Our influence has its foundation in the relationships we build.

difference between parenting and influencing. As parents, we guide our kids until adulthood; after that, it's about influencing. And it's the same with adults around us. Our influence has its foundation in the relationships we build. If God nudges you to offer some wisdom-filled correction to another adult, their ability to really hear it is tied to the quality of your connection with them. So if God gives you a correctional word to offer to an adult, the chances that they can hear the word are partly dependent on how much you have already invested in your relationship with them.

Let's get real about this truth for a moment. God does not hold us responsible for the behavior of other adults. We are responsible *to* them as brothers and sisters in Christ, but we are not responsible *for* them, as we are with children. Can I just get an amen to that? You don't have to lose sleep because an adult in your life made a bad decision and you couldn't persuade them not to.

Through parenting I also learned that the correctional word doesn't shame anyone. When I correct my kids, I don't do it publicly. I don't call them out because I feel embarrassed about their behavior. I don't put the embarrassment on them to compel them to act right. Likewise, in my position of leadership I sometimes need to give feedback to people who are under my care. As with my kids, my priority is to protect my connection to their heart, which preserves my ability to let God use me to influence their lives. So I take time. I wait for an appropriate private moment to talk with them. I look them in the eye and communicate. I honor and respect their dignity, because I believe this is how God treats us.

If you don't have an established relationship of trust with someone and can't offer them privacy and dignity, you'll undermine your influence and they won't hear the word. In that case it's better to pray that God will send someone who does have influence to give

ANSWERS TO LINGERING QUESTIONS

the person the correction. Leave it alone and trust God to care for the situation.

WHAT DOES IT MEAN IF GOD SEEMS SILENT?

Once you learn how God speaks to you through your Prophetic Personality, you'll find that He is rarely silent. You're likely to experience Him speaking to you far more often than before! When we are listening, we encounter Him all the time.

But those of us who have been in a relationship with the Lord for a while know that something else is also true: Sometimes the Holy Spirit gives us a specific word to live on for a long time. While we continue to read God's Word, stay in community, and get good teaching, we know we're living on a particular word, and we're going to do that until God interrupts it or gives us something else. God doesn't tell us every little thing. He tells us only what we need to know. If you don't have a clear sense that God is giving you an urgent word or immediate action to take, don't go to the default belief that you've done something wrong or lost His favor. Imagine this: When you've got that deep knowing that someone truly cares for you, their quiet moments aren't some kind of disconnect signal. Nope, it's quite the opposite—it's a surefire sign of connection. It's like this cozy space where you're totally at ease, just being there, side by side, in that peaceful hush.

As many pastors have said: "When you don't know what to do next, just keep on doing the last thing He told you to do." God might be inviting you to obey and grow until He is ready to reveal what's next. Don't shortcut this process or question its importance in your life.

We need time to cultivate the fruit of the Spirit. It doesn't happen overnight. When we receive Christ, God replaces our habits of the flesh with His fruit—instead of anger, we have peace—but it's a seed that needs to grow. Trust that it will flourish in due time, if you're faithful to do what God has put in front of you. "For the one who sows to his own flesh will from the flesh reap corruption, but the one who sows to the Spirit will from the Spirit reap eternal life. And let us not grow weary of doing good, for in due season we will reap, if we do not give up" (Gal. 6:8–9 ESV).

WHERE CAN I FIND MORE RESOURCES ON LISTENING TO GOD?

- Visit truthtotable.com to take the free Prophetic Personalities quiz and purchase the eight-week video course, which has a downloadable workbook that takes you deeper into the concepts offered in this book. You can complete the course independently or with a group.
- Visit the store at Bethel Church (shop.bethel.com) and search "hearing God" for books, workbooks, and downloadable teachings about how God speaks to us.
- Read *Whisper: How to Hear the Voice of God* by Mark Batterson.
- Read *Hearing from God: Five Steps to Knowing His Will for Your Life* by David Stine. The book includes a guided forty-day devotional.
- Read *Can You Hear Me? Tuning In to the God Who Speaks* by Brad Jersak.

THE POWER OF CONNECTION WITH GOD

With all wisdom and understanding, he made known
to us the mystery of his will according to his good
pleasure, which he purposed in Christ, to be put into
effect when the times reach their fulfillment—to bring
unity to all things in heaven and on earth under Christ.

–EPHESIANS 1:8–10

EARLY ONE MORNING MY PHONE BUZZED, AND I PICKED
up my phone to read the text.

> Havilah, would you be willing to come minister prophetically
> to a VIP today?

Trying to wake myself up, I reread the message, then read it out
loud to Ben, who was lying in bed beside me.

We agreed this would be a good thing to do. We quickly threw on our clothes and drove to the private location we were given. The host met us at the electric gate. We rolled down our window to ask him what to do next, and he explained that Ben would not be allowed to go with me and the host would need to take my phone. It all happened so fast that we didn't have time to question. Ben climbed out of the car, and I drove up the hill solo.

I didn't know what I was walking into or who I was about to meet. I'd never been asked to do anything like this before. When I got to the house at the top of the hill, I awkwardly gathered my coffee and keys and climbed out of the car. A woman met me and walked me beyond the main house to a smaller home on the property. She took me to a back room, explaining she'd return shortly.

While I waited, my mind began to wander. Who would be walking through the door? I secretly hoped to meet Oprah. What can I say? I'm a nineties girl! Maybe Dr. Phil would be right behind her, carrying her coffee.

The possibility delighted me. Then a fearful thought interrupted. What if I had no idea who this person was? Would I have to fake my way through the introduction? What if it was a famous athlete? My sons would mock me for the rest of my life. "Mom, *everyone* in the world knows who that is!" Except for their dumb mom. I grinned, imagining their teasing.

The door opened and two women entered—the one who had brought me and another I immediately recognized and had not expected. My brain kicked into overdrive.

I tried to merge the person standing in front of me with the person in my head. Full disclosure: I'm a little too old to know much about her story. I'm sure if you had caught me a decade earlier, I might have been a fan girl. As I stood there, I felt much more like a mother than a peer. She was covered head to toe in a hoodie with the hood up, sweatpants, and thick socks. We awkwardly greeted each other. It was clear that she was guarded, and for a good reason. Her fragility struck me.

She was human. A much smaller human than I'd imagined.

The host directed us to our seats, then I slowly explained my hope for our time together. I would pray for her. I would ask God what He wanted to say to her, and she didn't need to do anything. She could just experience it without any expectations. She looked as nervous as I felt.

My brain started to play out every negative thing that could happen. I imagined her jumping up, yelling at me, "What are you doing, and why are you here?" I imagined her bodyguards dragging me out of the room, throwing me in a car, and driving to an unknown location where the public would be warned to report any sightings of a middle-aged woman claiming to hear the voice of God.

I stopped myself midthought. I knew how to do this. I'd ministered like this thousands of times. Maybe not to A-list celebrities but to thousands of men and women around the world. And to God, aren't we all A-listers?

Calm confidence replaced my anxiety. I leaned into my spiritual muscle memory. I didn't have to try harder or sound more profound. I only had to do what God created me to do: connect with the Divine to communicate His thoughts and feelings to His creation, in this case His daughter.

I closed my eyes. Took a deep breath. A picture gradually entered my mind's eye; there it was! I knew enough not to try to process what I was visualizing but instead to communicate precisely what I saw—nothing more, nothing less. I shared the picture with her and started to experience more as I shared it. I saw more things. Then

I began to feel specific emotions. I knew I needed to say certain things. God gave me words and phrases outside my typical vocabulary. I didn't take the time to question whether any of it would mean something to her or if it even made sense.

My filter was simple. I was with a human being who is loved by God. She was just a girl, His daughter. She wasn't a celebrity to Him. She wasn't a tabloid headline. She was just a girl looking to God for answers to the big questions she couldn't answer.

After a while, I opened my eyes timidly. You never know how someone is going to experience this kind of an encounter. I never assume it's landing well. But it was evident God was speaking to her. She'd been crying for quite a while; her body was gently shaking. God was clearly speaking to the deepest part of who she was.

Moved by her visible emotion, I asked if I could put my hand on her to pray. She agreed, and eventually my hand turned into a half hug as she softened and fell into my embrace. I was vividly aware I was speaking words that only God and she could understand. I relaxed in the anointing. Like a runner with a runner's high, I was in the zone, interacting with the Divine, being a bridge for her.

A little over an hour later, we were done. Honestly, I don't remember much of what I said. The session wasn't recorded, so we'll never know. She stood up and walked out of the room with tissues in her hands. We haven't spoken since.

I'll never forget that day. Not because of who she was (obviously, I googled her to see if she was as big a deal as I'd thought—yes!) or because of the "you'll never believe what happened to me" story I could tell. (I told only a few close friends and I had to kill them afterward.) In all seriousness, I remember that day because I got to see the God of the universe lean in and speak to one of His kids in a way only a heavenly Father could.

After the girl left me, I climbed into our car to leave. Tears filled my eyes. I picked up Ben at the bottom of the hill and cried the whole way home. I cried a little because of the situation's intensity; I think my body needed the release. But I also wept because I was overwhelmed by God's enormous love and care for this woman. He loved her unconditionally and emphatically. He wanted her to know His thoughts on every aspect of her life. God is so generous! He wanted her to know she was His child, and she didn't have to do life alone.

She could be powerful because she would always have access to Him.

Just like me. Just like you.

You are here in this world, time, and place because God wants you here. He has things to say to you, to your family and friends, to your community, your city, state, and country. He has things to say to the world. Some of these He wants to say through you. Yes, you, with all your imperfections and questions. The world needs imperfect people, like you and me, revealing a perfect God!

The world needs imperfect people, like you and me, revealing a perfect God!

We need supernatural people—that is, those who allow the *super* of God to touch every aspect of their *natural*. We need people who believe without a doubt that they are created to hear God's voice.

We need people who possess not only intellectual intelligence but also spiritual intelligence. Sharp-minded people who understand how to apply God's wisdom and will in their lives. Wise people who love the Lord with all their heart, soul, mind, and strength.

We need creative souls who use their talents to showcase the beauty of God. Artists who can capture the essence of God's heart through their paintings, dancers who can express His grace through movement, musicians who can evoke His presence through music, and other creatives who can hear God's voice and use their imagination to bring His glory to life.

We need people who view God's voice not as a limited resource but as an abundant source of wisdom and guidance.

We need pastors who hear directly from God and preach from an intimate place of revelation rather than simply regurgitating information from a book.

We need worship leaders who are attuned to the Holy Spirit's leading and can flow with His direction, even when they're in the middle of a set list.

We need everyday men and women who see their workplace as a venue where they can share the voice and love of God when opportunities arise.

We need people who see God as a loving and willing communicator rather than a distant, angry, or disconnected being.

We need people who know God and feel God's presence and share that power with the world.

I hope that the time and money and attention and energy you committed to read these pages have given you what you hoped for. Before you close this book, I want to empower you to begin to put its principles into practice in your life by praying for you:

Holy Spirit, there are a lot of good things in the world, but if they don't bring us closer to You, then they are not what we need. They are not what the world needs. Lord, I pray that You would activate these gifts of listening and learning in the hearts and minds of everyone who reads these pages.

I pray for the Hearers, all those who are getting Your incredibly detailed play-by-play. Lord, write Your words on their hearts. If they haven't heard You for a while, open their ears for whatever new thing You want to give them, or remind them to hold on to the last thing You told them. Speak to them. Activate their hearing gift in faith so it might grow in Jesus' name.

I pray for the Seers, the visionaries. Lord, You give them big dreams to build things for Your kingdom, so all of us can step up to be who You call us to be. Awaken their seeing gift and give them Your supernatural endurance to bring about Your visions for the world.

I pray for all the Feelers, who sense Your heart. Lord, I pray that You would grant them discernment to understand what is from You and what isn't. I ask that You would give them a friend as faithful as Jonathan was to David,[1] a partner to help protect them and release the burdens that aren't theirs to carry. Allow Your great love to spill out through their hearts to the world.

I pray for the Knowers, those who have a keen sense of what You are doing. Please give them Your confidence to take themselves seriously, so they can release all confusion, all questions, all doubts about their spirituality. Give them wisdom for each hour, God. Affirm Your guidance in their deepest parts so they have no doubt as to what You will do. In Jesus' name, amen.

As we reach our final moments together, let these words sink deep within. You're created to hear God's voice profoundly and uniquely. Your special design lets you tap into His wisdom anytime, anywhere. I want to remind you: your life isn't just about you and your growth; it's about carrying His love and message to those around you.

So take these words as your call to action, your anthem of purpose. Embrace your uniqueness, listen closely to His whispers, nurture your talents, and let your life reveal His love. And don't forget: you can empower others by understanding and sharing your Prophetic Personality. Help them discover theirs too. This, I believe, is the key to us growing into a community of believers celebrated for our ability to hear God's voice.

ACKNOWLEDGMENTS

TO HOLY SPIRIT: THANK YOU FOR CREATING ME TO HEAR You uniquely and personally. I'm so grateful You found me. I can't wait for that eternity we've got ahead of us. Let's keep this divine conversation going!

TO MY BEN: The love of my life, coadventurer, best friend. Thank you for always believing in me and refusing to let me live small. It's been an extraordinary journey. From conquering intimidating peaks to building our own little family to embarking on countless adventures, God knew what He was doing when He put us together. The Feeler in you has a window through which I've glimpsed the tender side of God's heart, the tear-streaked compassion that mirrors His love. You've challenged me to push beyond my limits, embrace what truly matters, and find joy even during life's chaos. And let's not forget you are the funniest person I've ever met. I am forever grateful you chose me to be your wife. Let's grow old together!

TO MY BOYS, JUDAH, HUDSON, GRAYSON, AND BECKHAM:
Being your mom has been my most incredible adventure and proudest accomplishment. Your pure, wild, limitless love has transformed me. My prayer for each of you is simple yet profound: May you hear God's voice all the days of your life, guiding, comforting, and inspiring you to live the adventurous life He has planned for you. That you would embrace your unique ability to connect with His voice, to rise above the world's noise, and to know Him as an ever-present, always-accessible God.

TO MY SISTER, DEBORAH: More than my wombmate, you've been my trailblazing partner in this journey of hearing God. You embarked on this adventure from the beginning, showing me how to tune into the divine frequencies as a true Hearer. Your wisdom, guidance, and unwavering belief have shaped my path in extraordinary ways. It's an honor to witness the intimate perspective of your play-by-play conversations with God. Thank you for being a pioneer with me all those years ago.

TO MY MOM AND DAD: From my earliest memories, you've been molding my spiritual path and introducing me to the voice of God. Your journey has been a living testament to the power of hearing His voice, and I'm forever grateful for your guidance, example, and unwavering faith. You've shown me what it means to follow Jesus wholeheartedly, and I can't thank you enough.

TO MY LOCAL GIRLFRIENDS: You're the ultimate spiritual girl gang. I'm beyond grateful for each of you. Through your daily choices, you've beautifully demonstrated what it means to hear the voice of God individually and collectively. Your presence in my life has been a constant source of support, inspiration, and intimacy. I've learned the most about what it looks like to hear God daily from you.

TO HOLLY: You're a powerhouse, no doubt about it. Thanks for being the driving force that pushed me to record this message and transform it into something extraordinary. Your belief in this mission has opened doors I never knew existed, and because of you, countless people have heard God's voice in a whole new way.

TO KRIS VALLOTTON: My friend, your unwavering belief in me and my capacity to hear God has been a cornerstone of my journey. You've played a significant role in guiding me to keep showing up, speaking out, and ensuring that my voice is necessary.

TO MY TRUTH TO TABLE COMMUNITY: TTT staff, podcast listeners, Insta and Facebook friends, Truth Academy students, and Author School scholars, thank you for your unwavering support. Every single note, post, heart, like, follow, share, and virtual hug has breathed life into my journey. Your belief in me and my message has been a driving force. *Let's hang out in eternity together!*

TO MY FAMILY, BETHEL CHURCH: You're more than a community; you're a sanctuary where miracles and the impossible become reality. Your faith and love have provided me a fortress of faith—a source of healing, support, and love. I'm honored to serve alongside each of you.

TO LISA JACKSON: From day one, your unwavering dedication to this message has been unparalleled. Your relentless advocacy, encouragement, and steadfast commitment to helping get this message out of my heart and into the world has been miraculous. You've transcended the role of an agent, becoming a prophet and a defender of the dream, helping deliver God's message to His people.

TO JANET TALBERT: My editor and writing warrior. Your determination to figure it out from afar has been a true gift. Your guidance and commitment as my editor have been invaluable, shaping this message into its best form. Thank you for being patient, persistent, and passionate about this message. We finally did it!

TO MY PUBLISHING PIONEERS AT THOMAS NELSON: Kathryn Notestine, Kristen Golden, Lisa Beech, Christopher Sigfrids, Mallory Collins, and Meg Schmidt. Your unwavering belief in me and this message has been a testament to your dedication. Your investment of resources to ensure this message reaches the hands of readers speaks volumes of your passion and vision. I pray this message travels as far and wide as your belief in me. Thank you for helping me!

NOTES

Chapter 1: Why Can't I Hear God?

1. I've written a more detailed account of this experience in my book *Stronger Than the Struggle*.

2. John Mark Comer, "There's No Difference Between 'Spiritual' and 'Secular,'" *Relevant Magazine*, June 16, 2021, http://relevantmagazine.com/god/worldview/theres-no-difference-between-spiritual-and-secular.

Chapter 2: Does It Matter If I Hear God or Not?

1. Julianne Holt-Lunstad, Timothy B. Smith, and J. Bradley Layton, "Social Relationships and Mortality Risk: A Meta-Analytic Review," *PLOS Medicine* 7, no. 7 (July 2010): e1000316, https://doi.org/10.1371/journal.pmed.1000316.

2. "What Happens in Your Body When You're Lonely," Cleveland Clinic, February 23, 2018, https://health.clevelandclinic.org/what-happens-in-your-body-when-youre-lonely/. Also Maggie Wooll,

"You Know You Need Human Connection. Here's How to Achieve It," *BetterUp* (blog), November 17, 2021, https://www.betterup.com /blog/human-connection.

3. Jeff Levin, "God, Love, and Health: Findings from a Clinical Study," *Review of Religious Research* 42, no. 3 (March 2001): 277–93, https:// doi.org/10.2307/3512570.

Chapter 3: What Can I Do Differently?

1. You can read the story of Meshach and his friends in Daniel 1–3.
2. Counselor Gary Chapman coined this term in his book *The Five Love Languages,* in which he identifies five ways people prefer love to be expressed toward them by other people. It might help you to think of the Prophetic Personalities as the four love languages through which people experience communication with God.
3. Brian Rosner, "Known by God," Ridley College, June 11, 2015, https://www.ridley.edu.au/resource/known-by-god-2/.
4. Rick Renner, "Given by Inspiration of God," Renner Ministries, September 18, 2018, https://renner.org/article/given-by-inspiration -of-god/.

Chapter 5: Discover the Seer

1. John Loren Sandford, *Elijah Among Us* (Ada, MI: Chosen Books, 2002), 163, quoted in "Dreams: God's Favourite Mode of Communication," God Conversations, accessed June 12, 2023, https:// www.godconversations.com/blog/dreams-favourite-communication/.
2. Spiros Fotis Jr., "The Power of Data Visualization," Aegis IT Research, May 25, 2020, https://aegisresearch.eu/the-power-of-data -visualization/.
3. Anne Trafton, "In the Blink of an Eye," *MIT News*, Massachusetts Institute of Technology, January 16, 2014, https://news.mit.edu/2014 /in-the-blink-of-an-eye-0116.
4. Tania Harris, "The Power of a Picture: Why God Speaks in Dream-Visions," Way FM, accessed June 12, 2023, https://www.wayfm.org .au/the-power-of-a-picture-why-god-speaks-in-dream-visions/.

Chapter 6: Discover the Feeler

1. John Dunn, *The Great Evangelical Awakening of the 18th Century* (Blackwood, AU: New Creation Publications, 1983), 17, PDF, http://docplayer.net/42807020-The-great-evangelical-awakening-of -the-eighteenth-century.html.
2. *Merriam-Webster*, s.v. "intercede," accessed May 21, 2023, https://www.merriam-webster.com/dictionary/intercede.
3. Legendary intercessors such as Dutch Sheets, C. Peter Wagner, Cindy Jacobs, Joy Dawson, and Beni Johnson, just to name a few, have written whole books on intercessory prayer. I urge you to read them.
4. Oswald Chambers, "Holiness or Hardiness Toward God?," *My Utmost for His Highest*, accessed May 21, 2023, https://utmost.org /holiness-or-hardness-toward-god/.
5. David Guzik, "This work of casting can be so difficult . . . ," Enduring Word, Facebook photo post, July 25, 2021, https://www .facebook.com/EnduringWordCommentary/photos/a.945334655537 739/5769974393073717/?type=3.

Chapter 7: Discover the Knower

1. *Merriam-Webster*, s.v. "intuition," accessed May 21, 2023, https://www.merriam-webster.com/dictionary/intuition.
2. Christina Dronen, "The Mystery of Mother's Intuition Revealed in the Bible," Gentle Christian Parenting, January 11, 2021, https://gentlechristianparenting.com/mothers-intuition/.
3. Ilse Kleyn, "The Spirit of Wisdom," Art of Kleyn, accessed June 12, 2023, https://www.artofkleyn.co.za/pop%2023%2012.html.
4. A. W. Tozer, *The Pursuit of God: The Human Thirst for the Divine* (1948; repr., Chicago: Moody Publishers, 2015), 72, 73.

Chapter 9: Develop the Hearer

1. "Denzel Washington: WebExclusive," *ESSENCE*, updated October 29, 2020, https://www.essence.com/news/denzel-washington-webexclusive/.
2. Elena Tafone, "The Prophecy That Foretold Denzel Washington's Path," *Guideposts*, accessed June 12, 2023, https://guideposts.org

/angels-and-miracles/miracles/gods-grace/the-prophecy-that
-foretold-denzel-washingtons-path/.

Chapter 10: Develop the Seer

1. *Merriam-Webster*, s.v. "disillusioned," accessed May 21, 2023,
   https://www.merriam-webster.com/dictionary/disillusioned.
2. Benjamin Hardy, "Accountability Partners Are Great. But 'Success'
   Partners Will Change Your Life," *Medium*, January 17, 2019,
   https://medium.com/@benjaminhardy/accountability-partners-are
   -great-but-success-partners-will-change-your-life-8850ac0efa04.

Chapter 11: Develop the Feeler

1. Tracy Brower, "Empathy Is the Most Important Leadership Skill
   According to Research," *Forbes*, September 19, 2021, https://www
   .forbes.com/sites/tracybrower/2021/09/19/empathy-is-the-most
   -important-leadership-skill-according-to-research/?sh=42d30b1d3dc5.
2. Brené Brown, *Atlas of the Heart* (New York: Random House, 2021),
   118–20.

Chapter 12: Develop the Knower

1. Anna Katharina Schaffner, "What Is Humility & Why Is It
   Important? (Incl. Examples)," Positive Psychology, August 27, 2020,
   https://positivepsychology.com/humility/.

Chapter 15: The Power of Connection with God

1. Friends Jonathan and David forged a covenant promise to protect
   one another and their descendants (1 Sam. 20).

ABOUT THE AUTHOR

HAVILAH CUNNINGTON IS A SOUGHT-AFTER COMMUNICATOR, author, and top-rated podcaster, and she has been in full-time ministry for twenty-five years. In addition to being the women's pastor at Bethel Church, she and her husband, Ben, lead a nonprofit called Truth to Table. They're obsessed with reaching the world with Bible studies, messages, and lifestyle leadership tools. Havilah is the author of *Stronger Than the Struggle* and a dozen self-published Bible studies. She resides in Redding, California, with her husband, four sons, and two dogs.

RESOURCES &
NEXT STEPS

HAVILAH'S BOOK

Stronger Than The Struggle

RESOURCES TO GROW EVERY DAY

HAVILAH'S ONLINE COURSES

Development

Discover your gifts and steward your calling

* Prophetic Personalities
* Purpose
* Parenting Sexuality
* Moms Of Men

Inspiration

Guided studies to grow you in God's Word

* I Do Boundaries
* I Do Hard Things
* Leap Into Love
* Eat, Pray, Hustle
* Soul Food
* Radical Growth
* The Good Stuff
* More!

Influence

Crash courses to communication

* Writing A Book
* Delivering A Message
* Message Prep
* Going Live Simplified

Find all this and more at

shop.truthtotable.com

JOIN MY TEXT FAMILY!

Text GROW to
844-593-0473
to join for FREE!

Get text encouragements, spiritual activations, and free resources for spiritual growth and everyday truth directly from me.

STAY CONNECTED

Website & Newsletter
HAVILAHCUNNINGTON.COM

Instagram
@HAVILAHCUNNINGTON

Facebook
/MRSHAVILAH

Home with Havilah Podcast
HAVILAHCUNNINGTON.COM/PODCAST-ARCHIVE

Ministry
TRUTHTOTABLE.COM